SEARCH
The Graphics Web Guide

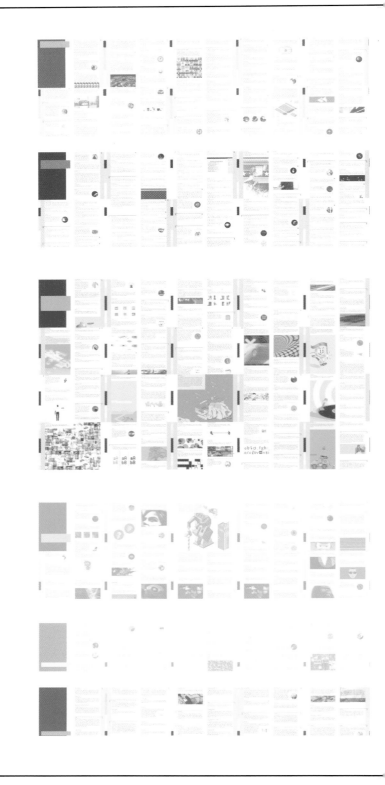

SEARCH
The Graphics Web Guide

Interface · Typography · Illustration · Photography · Animation · Film & Video

Ken Coupland

UNIVERSE

First published in the United States of America
in 2002 by UNIVERSE PUBLISHING
A Division of Rizzoli International Publications, Inc.
300 Park Avenue South
New York, NY 10010

Distributed to the U.S. trade by St. Martin's Press,
New York

This book was produced by Laurence King
Publishing Ltd, London

A number of entries in the current volume originally appeared in slightly different form in *Critique*
and *Metropolis* magazines.

ISBN 0-7893-0779-0
Designed by Tom Hobbs
Printed in Hong Kong

02 03 04 05 / 10 9 8 7 6 5 4 3 2 1

ACKNOWLEDGEMENTS

I am indebted to Jo Lightfoot of Laurence King Publishing for steering the project. At *Metropolis* magazine, where "Screen Space" has appeared for the last two years, my thanks to Horace Havemeyer III, publisher, for giving the project his blessing; to Paul Makovsky, senior editor, for pointing me to sources I would never have stumbled upon myself; and to Martin Pedersen, executive editor, for his advice and guidance over the years. Thanks also to Tom Hobbs, the book's designer, for his keen understanding of the project; Blanche Brann, my agent, for her support and friendship; and to friends and designers Erik Adigard, Laurence Arcadias, Peter Comitini, Guthrie Dolin, Amy Franceschini, Layng Martine, Patricia McShane, David Peters, Dav Rauch, Len Stein and Laetitia Wolff, for their suggestions and encouragement.

- *K.C.*

CONTENTS

Adam · Adams Morioka · Adbusters · Adobe Magazine · Adobe Systems · Advance for Design · After Effects Film Festival · AIGA Conference on Design for Film and Television · Alphabets, Inc. · Alt77 · The American Center for Design · American Film Institute · American Institute of Graphic Arts · American Society for Information Science & Technology · Ames Brothers · Ana Nova · Antidot · Appetite Engineers · Apple Masters · Apply · Argus Center for Information Architecture · Arkitip · Ars Electronica · Art and Culture · Art Center College of Design · Art Directors Club · Art Museum Network · ArtByte · Arts & Letters Daily · Ask Tog · Aspen International Design Conference · Association of Independent Video and Filmmakers · Association of Professional Design Firms · Atlas of Cyberspace · Atom Films · Attik · Autotroph · Axis · Babel · Clint Baker · Banff Centre for the Arts · Basel School of Design · Baseline · Saul Bass on the Web · The Bauhaus · Bauhaus Archive · BBK · Merrill C. Berman Collection · Peter Bilak · Bildbau · Bionic Systems · BIS Publishers · Bits and Pieces · The Bit Screen · Blue Man Group · Booth-Clibborn Editions · Born · Boxhorn · British Academy of Film and Television Arts · British Design & Art Direction · British Film Institute · British Interactive Multimedia Association · Brit-shorts · Broadcast · Broadcast Designers Association · Bruce Mau · Builder · Bulbo · Bulldozer · Büro Destruct · Cactus · Cahan & Associates · California College of Arts and Crafts · California Institute of the Arts · Carnegie-Mellon School of Design · The Office of David Carson · David Carson Design · Celery Design Collective · The Center For Media Sciences · Central Saint Martins College of Art and Design · Chermayeff & Geismar · Chinagraph · Chopping Block · Chroma · Chronicle Books · Cinematographer · Colin Moock · Colorbot · Combine · Comic Book Resources · Communication Arts · Communications Research Institute · Computer Arts · Concept Farm · Content Free · Shane Cooper · The Cooper Union School of Art · Cooper-Hewitt National Design Museum · Corbis · Cranbrook Academy of Art · Cre@teOnline · Creative HotList · Creative Planet · Creative Time · CyberWorld · Day Without Art · De:Bug · DED Associates · Deepend · Deleatur · Denmark Design School · Dept · Dept. 3 · Design and Culture · Design Archive Online · Design Centre of the Czech Republic · Design Council · Design DK · Design Exchange · Design Feast · Design Garten · Design Interact · Design Is Kinky · The Design Management Institute · Design Museum · The Designers Republic · Design®um · Design Films · Die Gestalten Verlag · A Digital Dreamer · Digital Experiences · Digital Media NET · Digital Thread · DiToy · Doors of Perception · Dot Dot Dot · Doug Chiang · Dutch Type Library · DV Creators · Dynamic Graphics · Eames Office · eBoy · Electronic Critique · Émigré · Etoy · Eveo · EverQuest · Experience Music Project · Extrabad · Eye · Eyeball NYC · Eyebeam Atelier · Eyes & Ears of Europe · Eyestorm · Faces · Factor Design · Factory 512 · Film & Video · Film Threat · Filmmaker's Collaborative · Fine Art in Print · Flash-forward · Flavorpill · Flazoom · Font Shop · Fontomas · For Designers · Force Feed: Swede · Fork Unstable Media · Form · The Foundry · Franklin Furnace · French Paper Company · Fresh Conference · Frieze · Funny Garbage · Fuse · Futurefarmers · Gain · Jesse James Garrett · Georgetown University · Getty Images · Getty Museum · Giant Robot · Giant Step · Gingko Press · Milton Glaser Online · Good Experience · Graphic Artists Guild · Graphic Design Gate · Graphic Design: USA · Graphic Havoc · Graphis · Green Lady · Guggenheim Museum · Habbo Hotel · Habitat 7 · Half Empty · Heavy · John Hersey · Herron School of Art · Hillman Curtis · Hi-Res · Hoefler Type Foundry · Honest · House · Houghnhnms · HOW · HOW Design Conference · Human Factors International · Hyper Island · I.D. · IFC Rant · The Illustration Conference · Image and Meaning · Imaginary Forces · Indie 7 · Indie Wire · Information Archi-tects · Information Design Journal · Information Visualization · IngredientX · Inside · Institute for Graphic Design · Institute of Contemporary Art · Interaction Architect · Interactive Design Forum · InterCommunication Center · International Animated Film Society Festlist · International Association of Web Masters and Designers · International Browser Day · International Festival

New Cinema New Media · International Professional Publishers Association · International Typeface Corporation · Internet Movie Database · Internet · The Internet Eye · Intersections of Art, Technology, Science & Culture · Intro · Introversion · The I-spot Showcase · J. otto Seibold · Jodi · Just in Space · Kaliber 10000 · Kraftwerk · Landor Associates · LaPuCo · Laurence Arcadias · Laurence King · Letterror · LifeF/X · Limn · LinkDup · Lineto · LiquidWit · El Lissitzky · A List Apart · The List · LiveArea · Living Surfaces · Loop · Lucidcircus · Lust · M.A.D. · Macworld Conference & Expo · Mad · Magma Books · Mappa Mundi Magazine · Mariot Hotel · Massachusetts Museum of Contemporary Art · MeCompany · Media & Beyond · Media Centre of Art & Design · Media Inspiration · MediaNews · Medium Rare · Memepool · MetaDesign · Metropolis · Metro-politan Museum of Art · Minneapolis College of Art and Design · MIT Media Lab · MIT Press · Mobiles Disco · Moccu · Modern Typography · Morla Design · Moving Image Gallery · Mr. Blowup · MTV2 · Museum of E-Failure · Museum of Modern Art · Museum of Television and Radio · Museum of Web Art · Mutabor · My Videogames · MyFonts · Myst III · NASA Earth Observatory · National Film Board of Canada · National Graphic Design Image Database · Net Baby World · New Media Centre · The New School · New York New Media Association · Nielson Norman Group · Nijhof & Lee · No Todo Film Fest · Nofrontiere · Nomex · Norm · Novum · Once Upona Forest · One9ine · OneDotZero · Orange Juice Design · Origins of American Animation · The Orphanage · Otis College of Art and Design · Pantheon Books · Parisfrance · Parsons School of Design · Pentagram · Phaidon Press · Photo District News · PhotoResource · Pictoplasma · Pixel Brothers · Pixel Surgeon · Plumb · Post · Post Tool · PowerHouse Books · Pratt Institute · PrayStation · Presenting Data and Information · Presstube · Print · PROMAX · Quickface · QuickHoney · R/GA Digital Design · R35 edu · Razorfish · Reala · RES · RESFEST · ReThink Paper · Retrofuture · Rhode Island School of Design · Rizzoli/ Universal · Rockstar Games · RotoVision · Royal College of Art · RPSONC · RSUB Network · Rustboy · Saatchi & Saatchi · San Francisco Museum of Modern Art · San Serif · Sapient · Savannah College of Art and Design · School of Visual Arts · Scopeware · Screenshots · Search Engine Watch · Second Story · Sensebox · The Sex Slave Decalogue · Shift (Germany) · Shift (Japan) · Shockwave · Shonan World Design Awards · Shorn · Siegelgale · Siggraph · Signalgrau · Silicon Alley Reporter · The Sims · Slamdance · Slashdot · Slo Graffiti · Smashing Type · The Society for Information Display · The Society for News Design · The Society of Publication De-signers · Soul Bath · Sputnik 7 · Stamen · State · Stating the Obvious · Steidl · Sticky Ideas · William Stout Architectural Books · Streaming Cinema · Studio AKA · Studio Dumbar · Super Bad · Surface · Surfstation · T-26 · Taschen · Tech Flesh · Tecknaren · TED · Thames & Hudson · Theory into Practice · They Might Be Giants · They Rule · Thinkmap · Thirst · Thousand Words · ThreeOh · Thru the Moebius Strip · Tint · Tolleson Design · Tomato · Tony Stone · Total Museum of Con-temporary Art · Trace · Trans · Trollbäck & Co. · Turbo Squid · Turbulence · Turner Duckworth Design · Turux · Twenty2product · Twin Palms · Two-thousandstrong · Type · Typebox · Typecon · TypeRight · Typographic 56 · Typomedia · Typotheque · UCLA School of Film, Television and Digital Media · Uiweb · Ultima Online · Understanding USA · Uppsala International Short Film Festival · Urban pixel · USC School of Cinema-Television · Use It · Utrecht School of the Arts (HKU) · V-2 Organization · Vbureau · Vector Park · Vectorama · Victoria & Albert Museum · The Video McLuhan · Vignelli Associates NY · Visual · Volume One · Vormberichten · Walker Art Center · Andy Warhol Museum · Web Page Design for Designers · Web Review · Web Sites that Work · The Web Standards Project · Web2002 · Webby Awards · WebMap · Webmonkey · When I am King · Whitney Museum of American Art · Wired · WM Team · The Wolfsonian · Jim Woodring · Writers Block · Xplane · Yale School of Art · Yale University Style Guide · Zed · ZKM Center for Art and Media · ®™mark · 100 Show · 16 Color · 2wice · 5K

INTRODUCTION

Like everyone else with access to the Internet, designers now have a wealth of information at their fingertips – if only they knew where to find it. Design resources are proliferating on the World Wide Web, and as they mature, their value to students, researchers and designers themselves can only improve. The design community – as well as general readers who are interested in design – could benefit from a comprehensive review of online design resources. Yet, to date, no single publication has offered an authoritative survey of the subject.

Search: The Graphics Web Guide provides a timely, multidisciplinary orientation to graphic design resources on the Internet. The organizing principle is a developmental model that follows the design world through its history, training and business aspects, supported by information on publications, organizations and related phenomena. Resources are listed according to category – discovery, media, practice, projects, groups and events, and services – and cross-organized by discipline – graphics (including motion graphics and interactive design), typography, illustration, photography, and film and video.

Search offers a selective yet comprehensive, illustrated reference work in the form of reviews of 500 Web sites of significance – arranged alphabetically by name within individual categories – which will be of interest to anyone involved with graphic design and related areas. Indexes and cross-indexes ensure that readers can access the most relevant information with a minimum of effort.

FOREWORD

Notes on Shelf Life

From its earliest times, through its headiest days, the Web has exerted a fascination for designers. While many who saw only its limitations protested aspects of the Web that were awkward and crude, others seized on its possibilities to fashion interactive, kinetic displays of information the likes of which we had never seen before. Today, the Web – rife with rampant consumerism and the wreckage of failed start-ups, while its creative applications grow increasingly ingenious and complex – presents a mass of contradictions. At the same time, the Web's potential for creative expression and as a research tool has never been greater.

A couple years ago, when I started writing a monthly column about design resources online for *Metropolis* magazine I had, I realize now, only a dim idea of the Web's potential. In spite of the years I had already spent online, "Screen Space," as the editors decided to call it, was to prove a transformative learning experience. As much as I thought I knew about the Web, what I discovered as part of my research for the column truly amazed me. Even more amazing was that the resources that I uncovered were very much a well-kept secret to other designers. Eventually I decided that a permanent guide – i.e. a book – was needed that would provide a comprehensive resource, but with a broader emphasis that extends to other areas of the design disciplines on which the column was focused.

Notice, I said "comprehensive" – and not, say, exhaustive. No way would I argue that I have mined every existing, noteworthy Web site of interest to designers. For one thing, this volume covers only what might be termed the two-dimensional design world (a second, projected volume will cover three-dimensional design – buildings, interiors, products and the like). For another, such is the still-exploding growth of the Web that new sites will no doubt launch in the time between completing this manuscript and the book's actual publication. By the same token, some sites will probably have fallen by the wayside.

At this point allow me to anticipate a couple of objections that have already been raised in connection with this project. First, as everyone who reads these words is no doubt aware, the Web has experienced a virtual tsunami of online failures in recent years. So how can a printed guide, given the delays involved with print, still provide an accurate view?

I would answer that, while there is no guarantee that every one of the featured sites will still be in existence at time of publication, those in question by their very nature are guaranteed a certain amount of longevity. In my experience the problem lies instead with destinations that linger on in cyberspace but do not update their contents. Either way, whether they're the personal creative expression of their owners or strictly not for profit, these going concerns have demonstrated that they have the tenacity to survive. As labors of love, by and large, they promise to be around for some time. Web sites that function as "hubs," linking to other sites of current interest (indicated by a large * in the text) provide invaluable information on the latest design developments.

If you know of a site you think should appear in future editions of this book, please let us know by writing to kcoupland@aol.com.

FRONT ■

DISCOVERY

History, background, schools, museums...

If you're looking to improve your cultural literacy in design terms, the Web today provides access to many of the same pathways to knowledge that already operate in the real world.

Design schools, with their relatively narrow focus, may not offer the same educational potential as colleges that teach design in the context of a liberal arts education. More traditional curriculums, on the other hand, may not provide the hands-on training and business learning that the successful graduate should expect.

Whether you're a prospective student checking out a school to see if it's right for you, or a seasoned professional just catching up on goings-on at the old alma mater, you'll find that educational institutions offering design degrees have universally embraced the Web as an effective fundraising and recruiting tool.

You can count on your fingers the number of museums around the world devoted exclusively to design, but those there are have been some of the earliest institutional adopters of the Web. Museums were initially reluctant to share their collections online for fear of widespread appropriation of their contents. Now they're leading the charge.

Museums have also become prominent supporters of Web-based art, contributing to the prevailing confusion between art and design. Just as photography has gained acceptance as an art medium, so typography and graphic design have come to play a greater role in the production of art – and nowhere more so than in the Web-based art supported by museums.

Curious about the history and development of design? Online encyclopedias are currently the best source of background information: to date, no other comprehensive sources have emerged. But a few sites offer specialized, in-depth analysis.

Adam
http://www.adam.ac.uk

Billed as "the gateway to art, design, architecture and media information on the Internet," Adam is an unassuming resource site that posts links to several thousand Web destinations carefully selected and catalogued by professional librarians. The site's internal search engine performed well enough in a highly unscientific test, pointing us to a favorite offbeat architectural museum. Adam does not, however, as a rule, source books or periodicals. We're still missing a comprehensive online clearing house for this kind of information.

Apple Masters
http://www.apple.com/applemasters

Blatant self-promotion for the Apple brand, this series of roughly 50 testimonials from Mac users who also happen to be well-known in their fields mixes interviews with scientists, adventurers and a smattering of design luminaries with squibs from celebrities (Jennifer Jason Leigh!). As you'd expect, the entries vary wildly in the quality of their commentary.

Ars Electronica
http://www.aec.at

Conceived as an interface of art, technology and society, and billed as the "Museum of the Future," the Center is based in Linz, Austria, hosting an annual festival that draws lots of media attention due to its provocative topics, canny choice of presenters and hip audience. Its Web archive presents significant art projects "from the pioneers of electronic art to artifacts in the digital era." A catalog archive includes a summary of texts from its previous publications that, the Center claims, constitutes some of the most comprehensive documentation of the development of media art in existence.

Art and Culture
http://www.artandculture.com

This "interconnected guide to all the arts" delivers a form of high-brow shovelware that covers a lot of the bases – with frustratingly brief biographies of around 30-odd graphic designers from Saul Bass to Paul Rand – but offers no new insights. It's one of those encyclopedic endeavors that are typically compiled by the overworked, under-educated content providers that have sabotaged so much information dispersion on the Web. This glorified data dump must be fairly new – many categories are laughably incomplete – and could improve as it builds out, but for now it's another one of those start-ups looking for a market.

Art Center College of Design
http://www.artcenter.edu

Internationally recognized for its applied-arts programs, the Pasadena, California-based college is a leader in exploring the digital and new-media frontier, with a commitment to the acquisition of solid traditional skills. The Center offers bachelor degrees in advertising, environmental design, film, fine art, graphic design, illustration, photography, product design and transportation design, with graduate programs in fine art, design, new media and critical theory. The Center's also famous for wholeheartedly promoting communications between the business community and designers.

Art Museum Network
http://www.amn.org

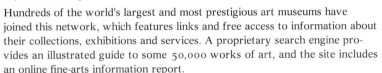

Hundreds of the world's largest and most prestigious art museums have joined this network, which features links and free access to information about their collections, exhibitions and services. A proprietary search engine provides an illustrated guide to some 50,000 works of art, and the site includes an online fine-arts information report.

Atlas of Cyberspaces
http://www.geog.ucl.ac.uk/casa/martin/atlas

If you can overlook its ugly design, you'll find that this virtual gazeteer – billed as "an atlas of maps and graphic representations of the geographies of the new electronic territories of the Internet, the World-Wide Web and other emerging Cyberspaces" – offers some absorbing visuals. The site posts "cybermaps" and links to other graphics that deliver at-a-glance visual synopses based on the constellations of statistical information on Web use. There's an Internet Weather Report with animated maps that vividly depicts "current Internet lag," and other maps that chart the geographical concentration of Web users. Multi-User Dimensions (MUDs) and other virtual worlds, and popular films that feature cyberspace as a governing metaphor get their due as well.

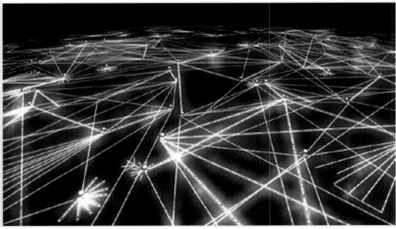

Banff Centre for the Arts
http://cee.banff.org

Situated in spectacular surroundings in the British Columbia Rockies, Banff has an estimable record of fostering the creative edge, and a robust artist-in-residence program. The Centre's Creative Electronic Environment provides advanced training opportunities in the areas of television, post-production, sound and interactive media production.

Basel School of Design
http://www.unibas.ch/sfg

A legendary crucible of graphic design talent, the school inexplicably posts no English version of its syllabus.

Saul Bass on the Web
http://www.saulbass.net

British designer Brendan Dawes hosts this multi-media tribute to the designer popularly hailed today as one of the founding fathers of motion graphics. The site includes posters and corporate identity by Bass, but focuses on his film title design, posting snippets of the films' musical scores and – what a hoot – an edit-it-yourself version of the famous shower scene from *Psycho* that Bass is thought to have shot for director Alfred Hitchcock.

The Bauhaus
http://nothingtoprove.com/bauhaus

This subsite offers refresher courses on people, places, products and philosophies that include well-written but all-too-brief cheat sheets with various links on Johannes Itten's color theory, and László Moholy-Nagy's graphic design and photography.

Bauhaus Archive
http://www.bauhaus.de

Research and documentation on the famous school is housed not in the original building but in a museum in Berlin designed by founder Walter Gropius. Billed as "the most complete existing collection focused on the history of the school and all aspects of its work," the archive is given a highly selective presentation at this well-thought-out site.

Merrill C. Berman Collection
http://www.mcbcollection.com

Displaying a selection of artifacts from one of the largest private collections archiving the history of graphic design, the site is notable for its sampling from the Soviet-era posters accumulated by Berman, an insatiable collector of modernist printed ephemera.

C California College of Arts and Crafts
http://www.ccac-art.edu

The college's design school offers undergraduate courses in graphic design, illustration, and a program of "design and media concentration." With a faculty drawn from the San Francisco Bay Area's thriving new-media community, the latter program "affords students with a particular interest in new media the chance to develop the appropriate skills and to contextualize the digital environment."

California Institute of the Arts
http://www.calarts.edu

Situated near Los Angeles, Valencia, California-based CalArts – while devoted primarily to the visual and performing arts – has a reputation for pushing the design envelope. A long association with the Disney studios has contributed to a respected tradition as an incubator for future animators, there's a graduate program in integrated media, and the campus boasts a top-notch graphic design faculty of creative types, many of them graduates themselves.

Carnegie-Mellon School of Design
http://www.cmu.edu/cfa/design

Don't be put off by the bleary snapshots on the splash page. Carnegie-Mellon has been in the forefront of integrating technology with design education, and the school offers an undergraduate program in communications design, and a graduate program in communication planning and information design.

Central Saint Martins College of Art and Design
http://www.csm.linst.ac.uk

The college has a distinguished international reputation, promising Britain's most diverse and comprehensive range of undergraduate and postgraduate courses in art and design.

Comic Book Resources
http://www.comicbookresources.com

This exhaustive archive and meeting place for hardcore funnies lovers and collectors claims a visitor count of 300,000 "unique fans" each month. Rife with insider gossip and sometimes painfully detailed interviews, Comic Book Resources is cluttered with visual noise in the form of banner ads, and comic characters only an aficionado could love. But the site's major draw – sure to keep you coming back for more – is a weekly-updated feature on one or other genuinely weird "oddball" comics.

Cooper-Hewitt National Design Museum
http://www.si.edu/ndm

Newly revitalized, this venerable New York City-based institution maintains its prominence with an ambitious year-round program of major exhibitions. The museum is particularly noteworthy for its huge collections of applied arts and industrial design, drawings and prints.

The Cooper Union School of Art
http://www.cooper.edu/art

The curriculum, leading to a bachelor of fine arts degree, has been planned to provide both a general visual arts education and a specific professional preparation for future artists and designers. The school's Herb Lubalin Study Center of Design and Typography comprises a valuable archive.

Cranbrook Academy of Art
http://www.cranbrookart.edu

Enormously influential in terms of the deconstructivist craze that swept graphic design in the 1990s, Cranbrook has a long history of intense student/teacher interaction. The school's emphasis on individual responsibility for the course of study has earned it a reputation for flakiness that belies its distinguished roster of alumni. Check out the hyper introduction to its 2D Design course, which promises "xperienc [sic] for theory."

Denmark Design School
http://www.dk-designskole.dk

The Copenhagen-based teaching institution is yet another legendary over-seas design campus that unfortunately posts without an English translation.

Design Archive Online
http://design.rit.edu

This "networked learning resource on the history of design," hosted by the Rochester Institute of Technology, draws on the school's 1,000-plus image coll-ection and supporting documentation to provide an informative account of 20th-century editorial design and photography. An exhaustive timeline provides a historical framework for the study of magazine design, and there is an ample list of portfolios – however the site requires a password to view them, without giving you a clue as to how you get authorization.

Design Feast
http://www.designfeast.com

An evolving and growing "webliography," this well-tailored hub is devoted to filtering the Web for potentially usable content on the family of design dis-ciplines: architecture, fashion, and graphic and industrial design.

Design Museum
http://www.designmuseum.org

Billed as "one of London's most inspiring attractions," the museum proclaims itself concerned as much with the future as the past, organizing a program of highly-acclaimed exhibitions "that capture the excitement of design evolution, ingenuity and inspiration through the 20th and 21st centuries."

Dia Center for the Arts
http://www.diacenter.org

For more than 20 years this well-heeled, New York City-based organization has played a major role in initiating, supporting, presenting and preserving projects in nearly every artistic medium. The site documents ongoing exhibi-tions at Dia's sprawling Manhattan headquarters, as well as long-term projects and ambitious plans for expansion of the existing facilities to new venues.

A Digital Dreamer
http://www.adigitaldreamer.com

It's not much to look at, but "the ultimate graphic design, Web design and 3D design resource on the Internet" links to over 200 resources, primarily sources for software that include a collection of free downloads.

Eames Office
http://www.eamesoffice.com

A family business dedicated to communicating, preserving and extending the work of protean designers Charles and Ray Eames, the office maintains a gallery and store in the real world. A helpful site promotes the Eamses' films and videos, houses several exhibitions devoted to their work, and posts selected short films on a monthly basis.

E

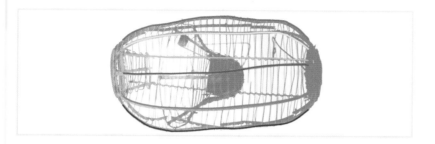

Electronic Critique
http://www.e-crit.com

E-Crit is a multidisciplinary undergraduate program offered by the University of Detroit, tailored to students "who want to combine creativity, critical thinking and technical expertise," that offers "tracks" in electronic commerce, programming and information architecture. The site posts scrappy analyses and opinion.

Experience Music Project
http://www.experience.org

Seattle's latest cultural minefield, housed in a newly-famed, Frank Gehry-designed behemoth, features interactive exhibits, "unique" artifacts and space for live performances – all created to celebrate the past, present and future of music.

Franklin Furnace
http://www.franklinfurnace.org

  F

Proclaiming itself "on a mission from God to make the world safe for avant-garde art," this one-time alternative art space went virtual during the 1980s art-market turndown. As the Franklin Furnace Archives, Inc. it now posts links to events and artists worldwide.

23

Georgetown University
http://cct.georgetown.edu

The University's Graduate School of Arts & Sciences offers a program devoted to communications, culture and technology, including courses in digital art and virtual environments. According to the site, "We believe that the current networked society – with the global convergence of communications, digital media and computing – requires a different kind of education. Knowledge from multiple fields must be combined to meet the demands of convergence, change, complexity, and globalization."

Getty Museum
http://www.getty.org

The 700-lb. gorilla of the art world is housed in a vast, newish marble mausoleum in the Los Angeles neighborhood of Brentwood. While mainly concerned with the fine arts and decorative arts, the museum schedules some design-related activities, and its Getty Research Institute quickly established a reputation for impeccable scholarship.

Graphic Design Gate
http://graphicdesigngate.com

As the name implies, this site provides a portal to graphic design resources online. Organized according to category (image banks, typography, schools, shows and organizations), the Gate posts a slew of links to quality information sources. The main page links to other portals and to magazines and e-zines, along with a miscellany of "odd, fun or good" virtual playrooms.

Guggenheim Museum
http://www.guggenheim.org

In a much-publicized effort to bring its public image into the electronic age, the venerable New York City-based institution has made the leap to the virtual world. Its facilities cloned in recent years to spectacular effect in the cities of Berlin, Bilbao, Venice and now Las Vegas, the museum has launched architectural renderings of "a morphing structure that is in constant flux." The online spatial study joins real-world interactive components installed at various museum locations.

Herron School of Art
http://www.herron.iupui.edu

An independent art school that's part of Indiana University Purdue University Indianapolis, the small (700 students) but cyber-savvy college offers a visual communication program covering design history, critical thinking, problem solving, typography and computer-related design.

Hyper Island
http://www.hyperisland.se

Based in Karlskrona, Sweden, this specialized school offers a two-year new-media program that promises "an environment where students [can] learn the new media industry in much the same way that one learns to ride a bike – by trying, failing and trying again until everything suddenly falls in place."

Information Visualization
http://www.pnl.gov/infoviz/about.html

The U.S. Department of Energy sponsors this no-frills presentation for all kinds of complex multidimensional data displays that utilize text, images, sound, voice and numerical data. Some visual analysis systems feature interactive elements that allow users to subset the data, run queries, do time sequence studies and create categories and correlations of data type. It's all wonderfully nerdy and scientific, and the graphics have their own unsophisticated charm.

Institute for Graphic Design
http://www.rotan.nl/mbo/grafisch

This Rotterdam-based school "is specialized in the design of all forms of communication," offering a range of courses from advertising design and printed matter to non-print products.

Institute of Contemporary Art
http://www.ica.org.uk

The London-based organization's New Media Centre is described as "a public playground for developing and presenting new and challenging work across the arts; for forging innovative ways of thinking about the wider culture; and for experimenting with the presentation of the arts."

InterCommunication Center
http://www.ntticc.or.jp

The nerve center for new-media experimentation in Japan posts a minimal calendar listing exhibitions, workshops and publications.

Intersections of Art, Technology, Science & Culture
http://userwww.sfsu.edu/~infoarts/links/wilson.artlinks2.html

The digital revolution has spawned its share of art-related phenomena, and this high-brow site delivers an encyclopedic overview of the terrain. Aimed at the intellectual hard core, the database surveys work by artists and researchers toiling at the frontiers of scientific inquiry and emerging technologies. An austere interface presents links to thousands of authoritative sources on topics ranging from biology, the physical sciences, mathematics and algorithms, to kinetics, telecommunications and digital systems. There's also a provocative section on information systems, surveillance and shadow corporations. It's not all brow-furrowing, either. The Barbie Liberation Front (remember the G.I Joe larynx swap?) gets due consideration, under "voice recognition systems.'"

L El Lissitzky
http://www.getty.edu/gri/digital/lissitzky

A couple years ago the Getty Research Institute mounted "Monuments of the Future," an exhibition devoted to El Lissitzky's astonishing career. The well-heeled archive only recently launched this online version, dedicated to the early 20th-century artist who helped revolutionize contemporary graphic design. An eye-catching introduction, sampling generously from the Getty's substantial holdings on Russian modernism, evokes the protean designer's signature style. Plentiful pop-ups display oversize reproductions of Lissitzky's typography, book designs and architectural studies. An articulate text reflects his recurring themes, with links to related documents and collections.

M Massachusetts Museum of Contemporary Art
http://www.massmoca.org

Housed in a renovated factory complex in a fading old New England mill town, MASSMoCA is a recent addition to the contemporary art space landscape that has emerged as a vigorous promoter of new-media projects.

Media Centre of Art & Design
http://www.mecad.org

Located in Barcelona, MECAD is a nexus whose activities are specifically oriented toward the research, production, support and diffusion for creative practices using "infographic," audiovisual and "telematic" media, and hypermedia.

Media Inspiration
http://www.mediainspiration.com

This self-styled "resource to inspire design professionals" boasts over 600 links, with monthly-updated content and new additions each week. Industry suppliers and vendors get their due, and a feature on "visual arts trends" posts a single timely link to various events and projects.

Metropolitan Museum of Art
http://metmuseum.org

Holding no particular brief regarding design, the largest U.S. repository of art and the decorative arts greets visitors online with a masterly execution of the display for its vast and varied collections.

Minneapolis College of Art and Design
http://www.mcad.edu

This well-regarded Minnesota campus offers undergraduate and graduate courses in design (with majors in advertising design, comics and cartooning, graphic design, illustration or interactive media), media arts (animation, film and photography) and fine arts.

MIT Media Lab
http://alberti.mit.edu/departments/media_lab.html

The Lab, building on MIT's reputation in a range of other disciplines – from cognition and learning to electronic music and holography – "has centered its activity around abstracting electronic content from its traditional physical rep-resentations." The Lab has helped to create now-familiar areas such as digital video and multimedia. Under founder and digital guru Nicholas Negroponte, this high-profile campus showcase has adopted a growing focus on how elec-tronic information overlaps with the everyday physical world. Well-known (and often criticized) for its pioneering collaboration between academia and industry, the Lab "provides a unique environment to explore basic research and applications, without regard to traditional divisions among disciplines."

Moving Image Gallery

http://www.movingimagegallery.com

Combining a physical art gallery with a virtual environment "in such a way that each is an extension of the other, and each a portal through which the processes of production can be explored," this New York City-based concern posts online discussions about the production of new art technologies.

Museum of E-Failure

http://www.disobey.com/ghostsites

The museum's Ghost Sites archives the logos of hundreds of failed dot-coms that unspool in rapid-fire succession – sobering souvenirs of the Web's Gilded Age. "May no historical revisionists ever claim that this wacky period didn't happen," the site's organizers proclaim. "These screenshots prove that it did!"

Museum of Modern Art

http://www.moma.org

Long identified with design, New York City's landmark modern art museum has recently experimented with various Web-based projects that seem to have disappeared – although they're probably merely buried – from its otherwise exemplary, fastidiously organized site.

Museum of Television and Radio

http://mtr.org

A national treasure, the Museum operates from facilities in Los Angeles and New York City, hosting exhibitions of dazzling depth and diversity. Online, "Perspectives on Television and Radio" features interviews with various personalities, viewable with RealPlayer.

Museum of Web Art

http://www.mowa.org

Dedicated to "the art, technology and culture of the World Wide Web," this flakily executed hub for miscellaneous online art projects conforms to the model of a virtual gallery.

NASA Earth Observatory
http://earthobservatory.nasa.gov

An extraordinary resource, almost all of which is free to the public, the National Aeronautical and Space Administration's service provides new satellite imagery and scientific information about our home planet, with a focus on Earth's climate and environmental change.

National Graphic Design Image Database
http://ngda.cooper.edu/index.html

Based at the Cooper Union School of Art, New York, this subscription-only database preserves and disseminates material related to 20th-century graphic arts and design. Designed to enable interactive and interdisciplinary analysis among faculty, students and the design community worldwide, it includes 6,000 digital images and data, compiled over several decades by designer and educator Lou Danziger, from the Danziger Collection at the Art Center College of Design.

The New School
http://www.newschool.edu

The New York City-based campus offers a graduate program in media studies with a novel approach: the master of arts degree is fully online.

Origins of American Animation
http://lcweb2.loc.gov/ammem/ammemhome.html

The Library of Congress posts fragments of its historical collections online, but most of the entries in its American Memory archive consist only of lists. A significant exception is this repository of early cartoons from the first two decades of the 20th century. Viewable, without explanatory text, in matchbox-size Quicktime versions that leave a lot to the imagination, the 24 shorts offer a tantalizing glimpse of animation's crude but beguiling origins. Highlights include appearances by Krazy Kat and Gertie the Dinosaur; Thomas A. Edison's "The Dinosaur and the Missing Link," a genuinely weird mix of live action and stop-motion; and "The Centaurs," a sexy, enchanting sylvan fantasy drawn by Winsor McCay, of *Little Nemo* fame.

Otis College of Art and Design
http://www.otisart.edu

This Los Angeles-based college has a reputation for experimentation (and a noisy, hyperactive yet agreeable online presence), and offers undergraduate degrees in communication arts and digital media.

Parsons School of Design
http://www2.parsons.edu

Part of New York City's New School University, the campus offers an MFA degree in design and technology "linking new and evolving digital technologies with the creative process [intended to] prepare its graduates for the new integrated design environment."

Pratt Institute
http://www.pratt.edu/ad/comd/index.html

From its main campus in Brooklyn, New York, and its Manhattan Center, the school offers courses in communications design with majors in art direction, graphic design and illustration.

Retrofuture
http://www.retrofuture.com

Images of space-age bachelor pads, picture phones, lifestyles underwater, rocket belts, flying cars, food pills and inflatable homes: you name it. This jocular site revels in recollecting all the forward-looking inventions that were supposed to change our lives for the better but were never realized, posting monthly features "where implausible and unfeasible plans continue to live and thrive, where yesterday's tomorrows are still in our future."

Rhode Island School of Design
http://www.risd.edu

At RISD, as it is familiarly known, "computers are natural allies in the creative process and the emphasis is on using new technologies to express artistic vision." The school offers courses in graphic design, photography, animation, and film and video.

Royal College of Art
http://www.rca.ac.uk

The only wholly postgraduate university in the world offering courses in art, design and communications provides what is described as "the best in pre-professional training." The school's focus is on project-based education with an emphasis on "face-to-face" teaching.

R35 edu
http://www.r35.com/edu

Promising "the Internet's only comprehensive, design-driven curriculum developed to help you succeed as an architect, designer or entrepreneur of the Network Economy," this slickly designed site offers one-year individual "courses" advertised to put students in contact with creative innovators and collaborators from all over the world. It is set up to work as a "live" question-and-answer message board.

San Francisco Museum of Modern Art
http://www.sfmoma.org

S

When a contemporary museum is just a few city blocks across town from the largest concentration of Web developers on the planet, you'd expect it to respond with a viable Internet presence. The Museum's crisply detailed interface carries forward its graphic identity while deftly organizing information for ease of use. The schedule for a museum the size of SFMOMA, with its many overlapping exhibition dates, is devilishly difficult to get across in print; on the Web, the site's overarching visual motif – a horizontal scroll – solves that task quite handily.

Savannah College of Art and Design
http://www.scad.edu

A relative newcomer on the design education scene, the College – promising "leading-edge technology in a historical setting" – offers a wealth of undergraduate and graduate areas of study, including graphic design, illustration, photography, and film and video.

School of Visual Arts
http://www.schoolofvisualarts.edu

Founded in the earliest days of TV as a school for cartoonists and illustrators, SVA has expanded to include humanities and sciences, advertising, photography and the fine arts, and more recently, animation, and broadcast and graphic design. A playful intro set to the words of Dr. Seuss enlivens the school's handsome and inviting recruitment pages.

Sensebox
http://www.sensebox.com/schools

Sensebox does one thing and does it well, posting direct links to all schools and universities – both U.S. and international – which offer programs in graphic design and visual communications. Using a website's hipness as a yardstick, you can quickly gauge the with-it-ness factor of a slew of schools. Although listings have been recently updated, it's a fallow area: the site once launched a monthly award for best design determined by user vote, but the last contest was held almost a year ago.

T
Total Museum of Contemporary Art
http://www.totalmuseum.org

Boasting the exclusive distinction of being "the first and most important private museum of contemporary art in Korea," Total is best known for its Web-based projects. Work by internationally known artists includes Chang Young-hae's mesmerizing word-based animation "Rain on the Sea."

U
UCLA School of Film, Television and Digital Media
http://www.ucla.org

Through its school – almost impossible to locate on its site – the University of California Los Angeles offers programs of study in the history and theory, as well as the creative and technical aspects, of the moving image. The school's Laboratory for New Media – good luck finding it online – provides access to industry professionals and their expertise.

Understanding USA
http://www.understandingusa.com

Information architecture guru Richard Saul Wurman has pulled off an ambitious undertaking, subdividing the sum of statistical information publicly available about the USA into 13 categories, then assigning each to a different design team. The published results, while predictably somewhat mixed, offer readers an unprecedented overview of a mass of otherwise incomprehensible facts and figures. A blatant promotion for the eponymous print version, the online edition is snappily presented (check out the sexy rollovers on the contents page). The only problem is that your computer's inferior screen resolution renders illegible most of the data in the text, giving you just enough to read – and frustrating you just enough – that you might even buy the book. Paradoxically, the site's very limitations actually make it a perfect promotional tool.

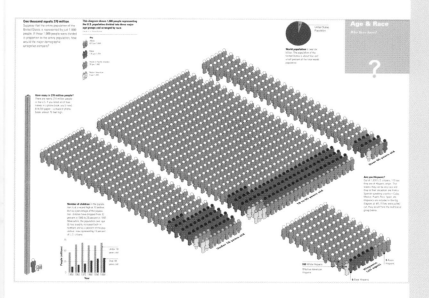

USC School of Cinema–Television
http://www.usc.edu

With divisions devoted to animation and digital arts, and film and television production, Los Angeles-based USC operates close to ground zero in the entertainment industry, offering undergraduate courses in animation, and cinema and television.

Utrecht School of the Arts (HKU)
http://www.hku.nl

This fabled college, offering postgraduate and professional education in the arts, posts an index of online publications and a multimedia section devoted to movies, animation and Web projects.

33

Victoria & Albert Museum
http://www.vam.ac.uk

A sprawling and variegated trove whose treasures span 3,500 years of the decorative arts, London's 150-year-old V&A houses 145 galleries that showcase the national collections of fine and decorative art. The breadth and depth of the museum's holdings places hefty demands on a website, which the V&A's online presence handles with aplomb. The site continues a trend among public art institutions to make Web access dependent on enhanced browser capabilities (there is no low-end version), while plug-ins allow extensive virtual tours of the exhibits.

The Video McLuhan
http://www.videomcluhan.com

This archive of videos-for-sale offers the most complete visual record of late communications theory guru Marshall McLuhan, in the form of rare archival footage never before available to the public that covers 40 years of his most creative and productive work. For the first time on video – and available only online – McLuhan devotees can view all of his major theories as he himself expressed them on camera.

Walker Art Center
http://www.walkerart.org

The Minneapolis-based Center modestly bills itself as "one of the nation's primary resources for contemporary art." Focusing on the visual, performing and media arts, the Walker takes a multidisciplinary approach to the creation, presentation, interpretation, collection and preservation of visual culture. Web art projects are prominently featured up-front.

Andy Warhol Museum
http://www.warhol.org

You have to wonder what the glamor-fixated father of Pop Art, if he were alive, would say about the location of his personal museum. Pittsburgh? But then, of course, it is Andy's home town. Besides, the Museum has distinguished itself during its brief history with a series of provocative, Warhol-related exhibitions.

Whitney Museum of American Art
http://www.whitney.org

Notorious for its highly influential but critically reviled biennial group exhibitions, the hallowed New York City-based institution has recently ventured into the digital realm with "Bitstreams," an ambitious survey that is fulsomely documented on the museum's site.

The Wolfsonian
http://www.wolfsonian.org

Florida International University's unlikely claim to relevance in the design arts rests with the Wolfsonian-FIU, housed in a landmark restored Mediterranean Revival structure in Miami Beach. The museum's splendor derives from its colorful millionaire founder and namesake Mitchell Wolfson, Jr. and his relatively narrow focus on North American and European decorative, propaganda and fine arts of the 1885–1945 period. The Wolfsonian's well-thought-out site, besides the usual exhibition schedule and such, boasts a wealth of visual material. Plentiful thumbnails of gems from the collection offer a tantalizing glimpse of its treasures.

Yale School of Art
http://www.yale.edu/art/areagdfrsets.html

The first college in the U.S. to teach graphic design as a discipline offers a two-year course in the craft – with a three-year program for students "lacking specific technical expertise" – as well as courses in photography, film and video.

ZKM Center for Art and Media
http://on1.zkm.de/zkm

As a cultural institution, Karlsruhe, Germany-based ZKM "holds a unique position in the world." The Center is organized to respond to the rapid developments in information technology and today's changing social structures. Its work combines production and research, exhibitions and events, coordination and documentation.

35

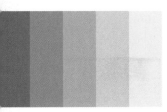

MEDIA
Publishers, magazines, forums...

Design, like any human activity, has its intermediaries, and every designer knows a few of them. Most book and magazine publishers and publications now have a presence on the Web, although it's fair to say that few have grappled successfully with its implications.

At first, publishers shrank from posting text online, because of a mortal fear that being able to read content on the Web would have a negative impact on subscriptions and sales. But attitudes are changing, and publishers are realizing that they owe their audiences that commitment. While there are still holdouts, the Web is increasingly perceived as a potent promotional tool – and that means giving readers what they're looking for, namely current articles, and more news and reviews.

Book publishers would seem to have the most to lose from the free dissemination of content the Web provides, a perception reflected in their relatively low online profile. But the Web also provides an unparalleled opportunity for them to reach new audiences. It makes sense for knowledgeable readers to be acquainted with publishers of the kind of books they enjoy, although traditionally that has been difficult.

More intriguingly, the Web has nurtured a slew of "zines" – exclusively online publications that are still finding an audience. Whether this volatile new medium represents the future of publishing – or the end of it – remains to be seen, but the prospects are certainly encouraging...

MEDIA

Adbusters
http://www.adbusters.org

Dedicated to nothing less than "reinventing the outdated paradigms of our consumer culture and building a brave new understanding of living," the Vancouver-based print magazine undercuts its noble intentions with unfunny spoofs and an irony-free critique of the media monolith. Its site generously republishes the print version entire.

Adobe Magazine
http://www.adobe.com

Effectively buried on Adobe's sales site, the online version of the company's print magazine is, confusingly, positioned elsewhere from other impressive but elusive editorial content regarding the Web and motion graphics. You can find what you're looking for by jockeying urls (thus: http://www.adobe.com/print or /web or /motion, followed by /features for articles or /galleries for portfolios).

Ana Nova
http://www.ananova.com

Fed up with all those robotic TV news anchors? Maybe you'd prefer a real robotic news anchor – you may even already have seen her on TV. Ana Nova is a "synthespian," or manufactured actor. Created by the British National News Agency, Ana was developed using focus groups to provide, in the words of her creators, "someone [sic] you warm to and whom you trust" while she delivers news and sports to your PC. There have been previous failed attempts to create a popular online cybersubstitute for humans, but Ana just might make it. Thanks to proprietary personalization technology, she adapts her demeanor to suit the tone of the story she's reporting; she frowns if it's sad, grins if it's funny, and guys will want to know that Ana should by now be available in a full-body version.

Arkitip
http://www.arkitip.com

This Hollywood-based zine posts ordering information for its magazine, posters and related gear designed with a "street" sensibility.

ArtByte
http://www.artbyte.com

This design-savvy New York City-based bimonthly magazine of digital art and culture samples liberally from its feature well, posting complete articles along with a wealth of visual culture tidbits.

Arts & Letters Daily
http://www.aldaily.com

Get that liberal arts education you missed out on in design school, delivered in manageable doses. Brainy and entertaining, the *Daily* samples from literally hundreds of newspapers, magazines and online services every morning, with fresh links to a half-dozen stimulating articles, essays and opinion pieces, and book reviews on myriad topics.

Atom Films
http://www.atomfilms.com

Now part of the Shockwave family, this online short film studio boasts an impressive track record of featuring numerous Oscar winners and nominees.

Axis
http://www.axisinc.co.jp/English_f/E_top.html

In its bricks-and-mortar incarnation, Tokyo-based AXIS Center for Design hawks upscale merchandise, luring shoppers and exhibition goers with its multi-faceted activities. The Web version regularly updates and presents news on the Center and its award-winning journal, and events highlighting current trends in the international design community.

B

Baseline
http://www.baselinemagazine.com

Unique among type and typography magazines for its full-color, oversize, print version, this British publication is stingy with its online editorial content, fudging with an electronic bulletin board of news, events and subscription pitches.

BIS Publishers
http://www.bispublishers.nl

The ambitious Dutch publisher of style-conscious design books – as well as *Items* and *Frame* magazines – posts thumbnails of sample pages.

The Bit Screen
http://www.thebitscreen.com

Maintaining that "The Internet's a new medium, and it demands new content," the service delivers first-run short films produced for the Web as well as Web-based serials of variable quality and impact, adding new programs every week.

Booth-Clibborn Editions
http://www.booth-clibborn.com

Titles from this classy, somewhat idiosyncratic British art-and-design book publisher are renowned for their outstanding art direction and superior production values.

Born

http://www.bornmag.com

An exclusively online showcase for art and literature collaboration, the Portland, Oregon-based magazine publishes an imaginative fusion of text, sound and image.

Boxhorn

http://www.design.fh-aachen.de/boxhorn

This student magazine boasts a striking interface but the text is unfortunately in German only.

Britshorts

http://www.britshorts.com

Self-advertised as Britain's newest short film studio (there are old ones?), it's a site "for like-minded people who love making, watching and showing great British and European shorts." Unfortunately, the studio catalog veers toward the mediocre.

Broadcast

http://www.broadcast.com

Yahoo's brave – quixotic? – bid to make the Web safe for broadband content features trailers, music video clips and the like. If the service survives – despite its portal clout – it'll be a miracle.

Bulldozer

http://www.labomatic.org/bulldozer

The Paris-based graphic print magazine posts a colorful palette and attractive backgrounds hampered by lazy type management, with no English translation.

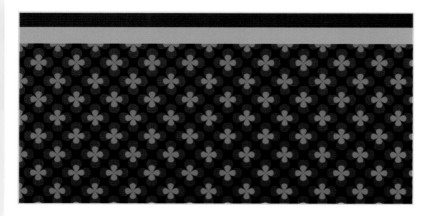

C

Cactus
http://www.cactusnetwork.org.uk

This British network's poster-format semi-annual suspended publication a few years ago, but is still worth a look for its edgy imagery and content.

Chronicle Books
http://www.chronbooks.com

This huge site advertises plenty of good design books, along with a lot of lifestyle titles.

Cinematographer
http://www.cinematographer.com

The online home for *American Cinematographer* magazine lives up to its claim to be "the premier online resource for the cinematography community" with in-depth articles, news and discussions.

Communication Arts
http://www.commarts.com

The U.S.-based design-publishing staple posts a selection of current articles and columns in their entirety.

Computer Arts
http://www.computerarts.co.uk

This British print magazine adopts a nuts-and-bolts approach to the topic, posting thumbnail software and hardware reviews, and cursory tutorials.

Cre@teOnline
http://www.createonline.co.uk

"The number one website for the online creative community" offers a British perspective on practical aspects of Web design, culled from its parent publication.

Creative Planet
http://www.creativeplanet.com

A clearing house for free, daily electronic newsletters of interest to the media community, this umbrella site addresses the emergence of the broadband Web and its potential for motion-picture production. The site's editorial thrust is that the explosion of digital technologies offers working Hollywood a host of career opportunities. A consortium of half-a-dozen titles provides breaking news of interest to creative professionals in directing, editing, post-production, television, cinematography, motion graphics, DVDs, special effects and more. Each mini-magazine posts current and topical news briefs, features and interviews, many richly linked to related information.

De:Bug

http://www.de-bug.de

Worth a look for its trim presentation of what is unfortunately German-only text coverage of music, media and culture.

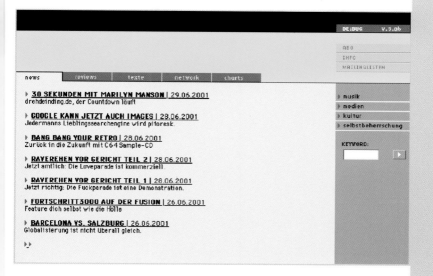

Deleatur

http://www.typo.cz/deleatur

This promotion for a handsome Czech graphic design revue redeems itself with timely topics, good pedigree and English translation

Design DK

http://www.ddc.dk

The *Danish Design Centre Journal* is up-to-date on developments on the nation's graphic-design scene, with short articles and listings of current events, most of them in English.

Design Interact

http://www.designinteract.com

A freestanding segment of *Communication Arts* magazine online that focuses on multimedia and technology, the site posts articles and interviews that deal with mostly relevant topics, but that conform to the *CA* reporting style – uncritical and naggingly uninformative.

Design Is Kinky

http://www.designiskinky.net

A cheerfully irreverent hub for breaking design news, cool projects and the like, the site hosts a discussion of relevant topics written each month by three different designers.

Design®um
http://www.sdc.sk

The house organ of the Slovak Design Center posts well-presented news and articles about current exhibitions and related developments.

Digital Media NET
http://www.digitalmedianet.com

Self-described as "the world's leading developer of B2B vertical online communities for the digital media industry," this busy hub supports 40 diverse "communities" serving distinct market segments: streaming media, video, animation, special effects, desktop publishing, imaging and design, audio, CAD, workstations, broadcast, post-production and game development.

Digital Thread
http://www.digitalthread.com

Trumpeting "the first arrival point for great design links," this busy-looking hub posts a gallery of Web design, a list of the best Web design companies, a library of graphic design books, links to type foundries, fonts, events, exhibitions and more. Listings frequently suffer from time lag.

Dot Dot Dot
http://www.dot-dot-dot.de

A somewhat forbidding site for the semi-annual magazine dealing with graphic design issues that has been given a stunning print iteration by Dutch designer Peter Bilak.

Emigre
http://www.emigre.com

E

Design publishing's best deal has to be this groundbreaking print quarterly's free subscription model. The magazine posts sample articles from each issue, along with ordering information for the studio's highly influential typography.

Eye
http://www.qpp.co.uk

Strange that one of the leading international graphic-design magazines doesn't yet have a viable Web presence. When we last looked the site for its publisher was still under construction.

F Film & Video
http://www.filmandvideomagazine.com

Besides lively but level-headed coverage of a host of topics related to the profession, this "digital media net community" pays close attention to independent filmmaking issues.

Film Threat
http://www.filmthreat.com

"Hollywood's Indie Voice" leads with mainstream movie reviews, but includes reliable reporting in the form of news and interviews on developments in independent filmmaking as well.

Flavorpill
http://www.flavorpill.com

A week-by-week listing of music, arts and cultural events in New York City, the calendar offers unsolicited – no paid announcements accepted – listings that are on top of the latest downtown trends and heavily hyperlinked.

Form
http://www.form.de

Online, the German-language, internationally recognized graphic-design print magazine is hip with the technology and posts fully bilingual content. Timely news stories enliven the standard ordering information.

Fuse
http://www.research.co.uk

British graphic design legend Neville Brody's poster-style periodical was still billeted with an "under construction" sign the last time we looked.

Frieze
http://www.frieze.co.uk

This well-regarded British print forum for art
and culture – and even a little design – posts short
articles about breaking art-world news.

Gain
http://gain.aiga.org

G

The American Institute of Graphic Arts' twice-yearly Internet-oriented report
on "design for the network economy" is only starting to build out, so it's too early
to say whether its desultory editorial content will expand or improve.

Die Gestalten Verlag
http://www.die-gestalten.de/verlag

Pranksters on the international book scene, these risk-taking German design
publishers have released a staggering array of monographs and graphics anthol-
ogies that are often light-years ahead of their British and American counterparts.

Giant Robot
http://www.giantrobot.com

Smart presentation of a questionable concept. The editorial content is clouded
by the kind of breezy boosterism that dogs so many online media startups. Message
boards on food, music, movies and travel – to the tune of several posts a day –
don't seem to be stirring up much interest. Maybe that's because the site's Robot
Lounge blog runs to inanity, profanity – or downright chicanery.

Gingko Press
http://www.gingkopress.com

A feisty newcomer on the design book scene with
an ambitious publishing program, the Germany-
based concern reprints Marshall McLuhan along
with originals by leading graphic designers. The
frankly promotional site goes deeper than most,
periodically featuring interviews and essays.

Good Experience
http://www.goodexperience.com

Usability *wunderkind* Mark Hurst posts daily commentary that monitors the online customer experience from a "holistic" viewpoint. News, reports and opinion on all aspects of information architecture make this one of the most beneficial places you can go for guidance on the thorny issues confronting designers who are concerned about how they interact with their audiences.

Graphic Design: USA
http://www.gdusa.com

The print version's bottom-line mentality is echoed in its no-nonsense posts: some industry news along with submission and subscription information.

Graphis
http://www.graphis.com

Promoting its books and magazine (the self-proclaimed "bible" of international graphic design of the same name), the publisher posts only brief synopses of feature articles from the current print version, along with news about calls for entries for its numerous book surveys.

H House
http://www.houseind.com

The online version of the print organ for retro font supplier House Industries which features pop-inflected design-related editorial content. The site posts brief synopses of each issue.

HOW
http://www.howdesign.com

Its print version is an industry staple, self-described as "the business, creativity and technology magazine for graphic designers." The publisher posts updates on its popular conferences along with the usual promotion, but no editorial content.

I I.D.
http://www.idonline.com

The well-regarded bimonthly covering the art, business and culture of design devotes a special issue to interactive media, but posts strictly competition and subscription information, and no editorial content.

IFC Rant
http://www.ifcrant.com

A feisty showcase for TV's Independent Film Channel, the site maintains a lively editorial presence online, along with occasional video downloads of interviews with indie cult figures.

Indie Wire
http://www.indiewire.com

Jam-packed with breaking news from the independent film scene, "the vital link for indies" makes good on its promise with exhaustive listings, lots of interviews and gossip.

Information Design Journal
http://www.benjamins.nl/jbp

In print form, an international refereed forum for theoretical discussions, research findings and practical applications of information design, the journal posts comprehensive, well-illustrated abstracts of feature articles on a range of abstruse but fascinating topics.

Inside
http://www.inside.com

Generating plenty of publicity with its exhaustive, up-to-the-minute coverage of media, books, TV, film, music and digital matters, this heavily hyped site abruptly shed its abortive print iteration and has since pursued an online subscription model.

Interactive Design Forum
http://www.awdsgn.com

Promising "ideas, resources and commentary for designers and design educators," a lone designer posts monthly updates with news, views, job listings and schedules of events related to interactive media. A stylish feature: graduated color bars that signal the relative popularity of different sections with readers.

Internet
http://www.internet.com

A portal for all things related to the Web and Internet IT, this network is packed with daily news features and calendars of events of peripheral interest to designers.

The Internet Eye
http://the-internet-eye.com

Despite its claim to be "the Internet's largest online design magazine," all you'll find are software announcements and reviews – but plenty of them.

Internet Movie Database
http://www.imdb.com

The premier source of movie information on the Web exemplifies how the Web not only improves access to information but transforms its uses as well. This exhaustive site provides universal cross-indexing of a host of cast, crew and production listings, as well as historical background. Here, for the first time ever, it's possible to read a summary, say, of a cinematographer's screen credits – a trivia buff's dream come true.

L Laurence King Publishing
www.laurenceking.co.uk

A London-based publisher and producer of high-quality books on art history, design, architecture and film. Its substantial graphic design list includes monographs by David Carson, Tomato, The Designers Republic, Attik and eBoy, as well as contemporary showcases and books on graphic design history for practitioners and students.

Limn
http://www.limn.com

This San Francisco-based furniture showroom publishes a fine magazine with some attention paid to graphic design. A smartly designed synopsis of the print version includes full reprints of feature articles.

A List Apart
http://www.alistapart.com

This weekly e-zine for Web designers is hosted by Jeffrey Zeldman, perhaps best known as the driving force behind the Web Standards Project, which fights for improved technology guidelines on the Web.

Loop
http://loop.aiga.org

An online discussion group dealing with interactive design education and available exclusively on the AIGA Web site, *Loop* is "an interactive, Web-based journal providing a forum for presenting research that illuminates and advances understanding of the relationship between practice and pedagogy in the emerging discipline of interaction and visual interface design."

Mad
http://www.mad.co.uk

 M

You'll have to pay an extremely stiff subscription fee to access information at this busy portal that focuses on design, advertising and media in Britain. The site displays just enough hints to the content to get you interested.

Mappa Mundi Magazine
http://www.mappa.mundi.net

Reviving after a long absence, the publishers of this richly decorated, exclusively online journal promise to examine "information discovery" on the Internet "via an eclectic mix of ideas about technology, history and the future of cyberspace."

MediaNews
http://www.poynter.org/medianews

Jim Romenesko's gossipy, up-to-the-minute coverage of the U.S. publishing scene frequently addresses issues confronting editorial design.

Memepool
http://www.memepool.com

Boldly proclaiming "your kinks, our links," it's a hub for guilty pleasures of the prurient and funky kind, served up daily by regular contributors who share an irreverent taste for the kitschy and off-beat.

Metropolis
http://www.metropolismag.com

The New York City-based print monthly devoted to architecture, culture and design includes some graphic arts coverage, as well as being home to Screen Space, the author's regular column about design resources on the Web. The site, which is kept current, posts selected feature articles as well as links to editorial material.

MIT Press
http://mitpress.mit.edu

The highly influential book publisher focuses on art, photography and design, with occasional forays into new media.

MTV2
http://mtv2.co.uk

The British music video TV network's showcase for work "created for and by individuals" makes a splashy entrance with a high-concept intro that offers what could best be described as a tectonic model for site navigation.

My Videogames
http://www.myvideogames.com

Advertising itself as "the thinking gamer's site,"
this smartly designed destination posts bimonthly
reviews with the aim of correcting what its creators
perceive as a popular misconception: that videogames are a mere cultural commodity undeserving
of serious review. "This lack of critical scrutiny
retards the development of the medium, which in turn
reinforces the prevailing attitude toward games."

N

Novum
http://www.novumnet.de

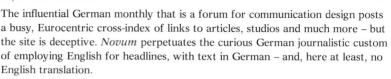

The influential German monthly that is a forum for communication design posts
a busy, Eurocentric cross-index of links to articles, studios and much more – but
the site is deceptive. *Novum* perpetuates the curious German journalistic custom
of employing English for headlines, with text in German – and, here at least, no
English translation.

P

Pantheon Books
http://www.pantheonbooks.com

Originally founded to publish European fiction and now a subsidiary of mega-
publisher Random House Books, Pantheon has in the past few years published
a spate of graphic novels, reviving a once-
struggling underground art form. The Comics
and Graphic Novels Center posts a remarkably
thorough archive of biographies, articles,
interviews and information on books by cult
favorites Chris Ware, Dan Clowes and others.

Phaidon Press
http://www.phaidon.com

The prestigious British art-book publisher has had a difficult past. Operations
revived in the 1990s and the roster now features a sparse but influential catalog
of design, film and photography. The finely-tuned site includes a detailed and
fascinating history of the firm.

Photo District News
http://www.pdnonline.com

An industry fixture in its print incarnation, the magazine has made a long and sustained commitment to its presence on the Web. The by-now-gargantuan site includes articles, interviews, forums, calendars, special multimedia features and an exhaustive inventory of resources.

PhotoResource
http://www.photoresource.com

Exclusively online, "the source for photographers" is pitched to non-professionals. The no-fuss site provides a commendable mix of news and reportage of interest to amateurs.

Post
http://www.postmagazine.com

Living up to its billing as "post production's business and creative resource," the print monthly fields news and reports on video, animation, audio and related technology, plus an editorial calendar listing the contents of each issue.

PowerHouse Books
http://www.powerhousebooks.com

Providing a home to some of the best and riskiest photography publishing on the planet, this relative newcomer on the book scene has brought some panache to the art-book sector. A no-nonsense site delivers the goods.

Print
http://www.printmag.com

The venerable U.S. graphic design bimonthly is typically stingy with its material, posting lead-ins to feature articles and departments from the current issue.

RES
http://www.res.com

R

Founded with the mission of promoting the digital filmmaking revolution, RES Media Group is dedicated to the art and exhibition of digital filmmaking. The outfit produces the acclaimed RESFEST Digital Film Festival and the bimonthly RES magazine RES ALERT, a media-rich e-mail newsletter which delivers breaking news on the world of digital filmmaking, important submission deadlines, upcoming screenings and events, video streams, product announcements and reviews.

Rizzoli
http://www.rizzoliusa.com

This prestigious publisher of books on art and design offers only password-protected entry to its site.

RotoVision
http://www.rotovision.com

Originally based in Switzerland and relocated in recent years to Britain, this publisher of educational – okay, how-to – books on advertising, graphic design, type, illustration, film and photography, with a focus on Internet design, joined forces recently with U.S.-based Rockport Publishers.

S

Sans Serif
http://quixote.com/serif/sans

The online companion to *Serif*, a German quarterly on type and typography, suffers from a severely design-challenged interface, but posts plenty of news and articles – all in English – of interest to type enthusiasts.

Search Engine Watch
http://www.searchenginewatch.com

As its name implies, this nitty-gritty site provides tips and information about searching the Web, as well as analysis of the search-engine industry and help for site owners who want to improve their ability to be found in search engines.

Shift (Germany)
http://www.shift.de

This wildly ambitious German showcase for experimental graphic design, whose print version continually morphs into varying formats (there's even been a video installment), displays a scruffy splash page that eventually cues you to an exhaustive catalog with English text.

Shift (Japan)
http://www.shift.jp.org

A Japanese "e-zine for digital generations" with a strong design bent struggles with an English translation for its hip, cosmopolitan content.

Shockwave
http://www.shockwave.com

An unabashed promotion for the software of the same name, the site posts better-than-average short films and animations, and a gallery of games.

Silicon Alley Reporter
http://www.siliconalleydaily.com

An unrivalled source for daily news and gossip about media, finance and technology in the New York City information industry that isn't immune from the boosterism that plagues so much new-media reporting.

Slashdot
http://slashdot.com

Unabashedly self-described as "news for nerds," this thread for geeks tackles the tough questions – how to get a game licensed, what the new trends in product development are, and the like.

Sputnik 7
http://www.sputnik7.com

Credited as "the world's first real-time audio/video Internet entertainment experience," this online broadcast network offers superior programming delivered via various departments: interactive video stations, audio stations, videos on demand and digital downloads. A lot of the best short-form motion work on the Web debuts here.

Steidl
http://www.steidl.de

This German publisher of edgy art books distinguished by their superb quality maintains merely a placeholder on the Web.

Surfstation
http://www.surfstation.lu

"Inspiration becomes innovation" at this chatty, relentlessly hip portal for predominantly European design exploration.

Taschen
http://www.taschen.de

This full-bore promotion for the German publisher of art and design, film and photography, and picturesque erotica includes a substantial catalog of forthcoming titles. The adults-only section is a must-see.

Tecknaren
http://www.svenskatecknare.se

Worth a look, this unassuming site posts material from the official magazine of Sweden's association of illustrators and graphic designers. Unfortunately, there's only Swedish text.

ThreeOh
http://www.threeoh.com

This tightly calibrated digital design journal focuses on goings-on in Britain but extends its reach worldwide, with a plethora of links, daily posts – and a resolutely hip attitude.

Trace
http://www.trace.aiga.org

A commendable effort to bring the AIGA's publishing in-house, *Trace* (issued thrice-yearly and sold on newsstands) is a smaller, more compact version of the old AIGA *Journal*, with the welcome addition of full-color photo illustrations, a less text-heavy feature well, and a distinctly edgy editorial spin. A stylish, and surprisingly legible, redesign by New York-based studio 2x4 notwithstanding, what jumps out at you about *Trace* is its savvily recalibrated take on content.

2wice
http://www.2wice.org

The virtual version of a much-applauded non-profit quarterly that frequently focuses on the offbeat, the site posts some of the magazine's current content with thumbnails and enlargements, and includes an archive with samples from past issues.

Thames & Hudson
http://www.thameshudson.co.uk

The British-based publisher of books on art and the decorative arts – with a smattering of design and photography – posts a catalog that includes a memorable series on international "street" graphics.

Twin Palms
http://www.twinpalms.com

The Santa Fe, New Mexico-based publisher is renowned for exquisitely designed and produced photography books with a homoerotic bent. Don't be put off by the clunky site, apparently created with off-the-shelf software.

Type
http://www.atypi.org

The online home to the *Journal* of the Association Typographique Internationale, an organization which hosts ATypI, the seminal annual typography conference, and publishes research, news and commentary relating to type design, typography, type foundries and typographic education.

Visual
http://www.visual.gi

This uninspired site appears to be the sole showcase for Spanish graphic design, with a selective directory of links to graphic designers, illustrators and photographers.

Vormberichten
http://www.bno.nl

News about design awards, competitions, announcements and reviews in The Netherlands, posted with Dutch text only.

Web Review
http://www.webreview.com

Exclusively online and self-described as "cross-training for Web teams," the largest and longest-standing weekly site dedicated to – and written by – Web professionals publishes new material every Friday, tracking Web authors, designers, developers and strategists, along with style guides, links and resources. "The bottom line? Real-world experience, and lots of it."

Wired
http://www.wired.com

The print version has long upheld a commitment to design, reflected in the content of its online daily reporting in Wired News (an addictive read, and the author's home page – make it yours, too!).

Zed
http://www.designstudies.com/zed

An online design journal intended to "bridge the gap between designer, student and educator," amongst other goals, the site boasts nice execution and thoughtful articles on a wide range of salient topics.

PRACTICE

Studios, makers, portfolios, process...

How designers go about practicing their craft is a topic of un-
failing interest – or at least it is to other designers. No surprise,
then, that most designers' favorite activity on the Web involves
checking out what the competition is putting up there. How
designers present themselves is at least as important as what they
present in portfolio.

If this book had been published a year ago, the roster of studios
would have looked a lot different. But that was before the Internet
economy underwent a cataclysmic shake-up. In the process, many
high-profile, big-budget design agencies that started up to respond
to the feverish entrepreneurial climate of the last decade met an
untimely end. These interchangeable entities – with their marketing
speak and tenuous grasp of design basics – will not be missed.

The landscape of Web design and development looks a bit different now. Many talented "creatives" in so-called "boutique" studios
who were lured into working for large Internet outfits have since
taken a reality check and returned to private practice, while the small
shops that stayed "lean and mean" by and large survived.

Adams Morioka
http://www.adamsmorioka.com

Espousing the belief that "clarity, purity and resonance are the foundation for clear, concise communications," the Los Angeles-based graphic design duo known for their tasteful whimsicality allow a playful Pop sensibility to come to the fore. A nicely detailed process chart provides as neat a summation of the client/designer dynamic as you'll find.

Advance for Design
http://advance.aiga.org

A laudable initiative by the American Institute of Graphic Arts (AIGA), Advance for Design's stated objective is "to establish a new community of design practitioners who are challenged to design for a world that is increasingly digital and connected." With its sprightly interface, the site's a glorified pitch for AIGA membership on the one hand, on the other a sounding-board that addresses the dilemmas facing graphic design professionals in the electronic age.

Ames Brothers
http://www.amesbros.com

Promising "full-bodied graphics with great flavor," these Seattle-based, street-smart *bricoleurs* promote their ebullient rock-concert posters, energetic snowboard ads – and actual snowboard designs.

Antidot
http://www.antidot.de

Floating horizontal rules enliven this typographic showcase for the various "flavors" of German studio Signalgrau, which includes an archive for the designers' delectable but, alas, dormant "Eyesaw" type portfolio.

Appetite Engineers
http://www.appetiteengineers.com

The Cranbrook legacy is alive and well at
Martin Venezky's playful self-promotion. This
San Francisco-based minor master of graphic
deconstruction proffers a deliberately un-slick
pitch with an ursine mascot that's available
in a "Grizzly" (Flash) and "CryBaby" (non-
Flash) version.

Apply
http://www.apply.de

The seminal type-design firm associated with David Carson's tenure at *Raygun*
magazine hawks its wares – scores of 90s deconstructed fonts that ought to be
ripe for revival any time soon – at a site (text in German only) that includes a
handful of photography and illustration portfolios.

Laurence Arcadias
http://www.arcadias.tv

One of the Web's premier humorists, the San Francisco-based animator archives
her frequent appearances on HotWired's Animation Express in an interactive
portfolio that takes aim at Arcadias' trenchant observations on male-female relationships and includes multi-path scenarios of love gone wrong.

Ask Tog
http://www.asktog.com

Fostering "human interface evangelism and practical design," Nielsen Norman
Group member and Apple GUI veteran Bruce Tognazzini posts a timely and
authoritative advice column that puts a designer's spin on usability issues, delving
into such thorny topics as the deplorable design of the Mac OSX interface and
the notorious Butterfly Ballot.

Attik
http://www.attik.co.uk

With offices in Huddersfield, London, New York City, San Francisco and Sydney, ATTIK at its low-key site strives to be "the world's most visionary communications company." The studio's business-like portfolio includes broadcast, print, and Web and interactive design.

Autotroph
http://www.autotroph.com

An appropriately gnarly promotion for TV, Web and print work by New York City-based typographer and graphic provocateur Barry Deck touts his agenda of "literate, pragmatic, idiosyncratic propaganda."

Clint Baker
http://www.clintbaker.com

B

Swimming against the prevailing stylistic tides, this Washington, D.C.-based illustrator crafts a quaint and anachronistic "portfolio viewing machine" to present a slim showcase for his wares.

BBK
http://www.bbkstudio.com

Hard-to-read text and fragile Flash implementation sabotage the presentation for this Grand Rapids, Michigan-based boutique associated with Web styling for furniture maker Herman Miller, Inc.

Peter Bilak
http://www.ui42.sk/peterb

Virtual home to work by the multi-talented, Amsterdam-based, Slovak-born graphic designer and writer, a crisply detailed portfolio features an impressive array of Bilak's posters and magazine covers, as well as a gallery of engaging QuickTime movies of his motion graphics experiments. Articles and interviews by and about the designer focus on issues relating to type design. Poke around and you'll find a kinetic display of the Eurotype project, a font "meant to be viewed at driver's speed."

Bildbau

http://www.bildbau.de/sign_for_new_media/default.htm

The smartly detailed showcase for these Berlin-based multimedia designers requires a bit of counter-intuitive jockeying – access to the English version was imperfectly worked out when we looked – but rewards with some well-reasoned rhetoric. "Multimedia does not exist for its own sake," they write. "Innovation does not mean the uncontrolled use of all available technical possibilities, but instead the search for new forms of implementation and means of expression, while remaining true to time-proven philosophies and strategies."

Bionic Systems

http://www.bionic-systems.com

An impressive demonstration for the talents of two youthful German interface designers, this promotion's graphic idiom should appeal to anyone who has pored over the visuals of too many space movies. With a whiff of futuristic angst, the Düsseldorf-based duo deploy an elegantly detailed GUI composed of deviously clever animations, rife with extraneous visual cues that play on the male-female dichotomy.

Blue Man Group

http://www.blueman.com

A brief animation provides a quick sampling of the striking visuals (remember the Intel commercials?) for which this music and performance ensemble – now Live at the Luxor in Las Vegas! – is justifiably famed.

Bubble

http://www.bubble.be

The trick to presenting a portfolio of design work online lies in providing a rewarding sensory experience that doesn't insult the user's intelligence. Bubble ("Put some in your media") obliges with a simple-as-can-be presentation, set against an eye-pleasing palette that manages to be both luscious and tastefully subdued. As you mouse over relevant areas, the interface – composed of contiguous circles that morph on demand into amoeba-like blobs – is constantly in motion, in an ingratiating display that lulls you with a soothing ambient audio loop. "Creativity rules," creative director Peter Dekens states. "So that kind of overrules our other rules." One rule Bubble ignores is legibility. The too-tiny, low-contrast type is a sure-fire prescription for eyestrain.

Builder
http://builder.cnet.com

A durable presence on the Web, tech portal CNET's Web advice column, promising "solutions for site builders," consistently delivers. Besides discussions, columns and reviews, the site archives a library addressing down-and-dirty aspects of authoring and site design, graphics and multimedia, programming and scripting, back end and site management, e-business and strategy, and careers and training.

Büro Destruct
http://www.burodestruct.net

Replete with in-jokes and free, downloadable interactive font showings, the promotion for these Bern, Switzerland-based conceptualists offers a chilly rebuff to the visitor.

Cahan & Associates
http://www.cahanassociates.com

The royalty of annual-report design divide their minimalist promotion into a photographic gallery of their workplace and a portfolio. An amusing collection of "rumors" anthologizes clients' pointed assessments of their talents.

C

The Office of David Carson
http://www.davidcarson.com

Saddled with the same moniker as graphic design's *enfant terrible*, this lone St. Paul, Minnesota-based designer makes the best of it with repeated celebrity disclaimers and a lively opinion column with lots of links.

David Carson Design
http://www.davidcarsondesign.com

Still a work-in-progress when we last looked, the online tease for the "real" David Carson's eventual Web presence was lofting some loopy graphics and a blog that wouldn't let us sign on.

Celery Design Collective
http://www.celerydesign.com

One of those rare studios that argues for sustainabilityas a factor in graphic design, this Berkeley, California-based agency aims to "integrate a deep understanding of ecological issues, alternative materials and manufacturing techniques into each phase of our design process."

Chermayeff & Geismar
http://www.cgnyc.com

Ivan Chermayeff's historic relation to modernism is his legacy to the firm's identity and graphic design, exhibit planning, environmental graphics and interactive design.

Doug Chiang
http://www.dchiang.com

A former Industrial Light & Magic creative director advertises his *Myst*-like personal book/film project, *Robota: Reign of Machines*, at this multimedia site.

Chinagraph
http://www.chinagraphny.com/china.html

A New York City-based post-production design and editing agency that specializes in creative film and video editing for commercials, documentaries, features and music videos displays a snappy presentation for its wares.

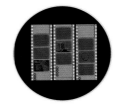

Chopping Block
http://www.choppingblock.com

A New York City-based graphic design house diminishes its efforts with an exceptionally annoying audio loop.

Colorbot
http://www.colorbot.com

Owen Plotkin of New York City-based Syncopation Films, a video editing facility, helms this chaotic but effective promotion. Fooling around with editing code and a vibrant palette, Plotkin and his henchmen craft an oddly effective communication of their production skills.

Concept Farm
http://www.conceptfarm.com

Deploying a slew of clever animations (note especially the distracting housefly) and jokey audio loops, the slick but hilarious promotion for this New York City-based advertising shop takes the agrarian motif and runs with it – falling just short of running it into the ground. Check out the Cud Cam on the virtual homestead's Live Feed.

ContentFree
http://www.contentfree.com

Lovely kaleidoscopic patterns segue to a cryptic interface that plays tricks on your cursor, making navigation tricky on this site for a Seattle-based studio that specializes in interactive storytelling with editorial content.

DED Associates
http://www.dedass.com

D

A British design consultancy with a hefty roster of corporate accounts crafts a grimly amusing setting – rife with elusive cues to interaction – for spare, Pop-inflected graphics.

Deepend
http://www.deepend.co.uk

There's a dreary predictability to many design firms' online self-promotions; not so the home site for this enterprising group of British new-media evangelists. The teensy, borderline-unreadable type might seem a bit off-putting at first, but as you mouse-over menus and the type morphs to a readable size, Deepend's minimalist interface gradually reveals its functionality. Further in, menus slice-and-dice the content every which way, so you get a look at relevant work you might not otherwise seek out – an appropriate envelope for the studio's impressive breadth of expertise.

Dept. 3
http://www.dept3.com

A highly calibrated treatment distinguishes this promotion for a San Francisco-based graphic design trio of dot-com refugees who specialize in cross-media branding.

The Designers Republic
http://www.thedesignersrepublic.com

Forceful execution distinguishes the portfolio for "brain-aided design" by this versatile studio in faux-socialist drag. There's a lively discussion thread, and a "Peoples Bureau for Consumer Information" that hawks TDR-related wares.

DiToy
http://www.ditoy.com

A German agency for Web design, e-commerce and "digital reality" posts static renderings of virtual reality elements, 2D and 3D product visualization, and active and interactive animations.

Dutch Type Library
http://www.dutchtypelibrary.com

The well-developed online home for this producer and publisher of digital type-faces features a brief but informative history of type design in The Netherlands and a catalog of a dozen classically-inspired fonts.

E

Eveo
http://www.eveo.com

Trumpeting the advent of a "new visual format," Eveo posits a user-generated content community based on the production and online distribution of eveos, "personal, engaging short videos" that the company syndicates over the Web. There has been a lot of talk about this sort of thing catching on, what with short attention spans, the currently slow-to-download Web, the indie film phenomenon, and so on. But take a step back and you can see that – even with a slew of budding Fellinis in tow – Eveo's is a stunningly bad business model (in fact, the company has recently pulled away from this approach). Online content providers are money-losers so far, and the audience for these fitfully engaging but trivial shorts is miniscule. A tasteful and distinctive interface encourages you to take this highly problematic concept seriously.

Eyeball NYC
http://www.eyeballnyc.com

This New York City-based "thinking design company" presents a portfolio in frames, sequences and QuickTime movies of multimedia promotions for an impressive roster of major clients.

Factor Design
http://www.factordesign.com

A top-ranking, bi-continental agency based in Hamburg, with an office in San Francisco, Factor posts a well-argued presentation of interactive assignments and other collateral for "using design to embody the strategy of your business."

F

Fontomas
http://www.fontomas.com

Here's a clever idea: every Wednesday, Fontomas posts a new font or dingbat collection presented in the form of a free, downloadable type experiment. The catch is it's only available for one week: as each new offering is launched, the previous entry comes down for good. The Essen, Germany-based organizers do, however, archive splash pages for previous postings that display a varied range of up-to-the-minute type showings from designers in Europe and the U.S.

Fork Unstable Media
http://www.unstablemedia.de

Hopping with spurious text and faux-techno flummery, the promotion for this Berlin-, Hamburg- and New York City-based consultancy bristles with wryly self-referential displays that are too clever by half, but that exude expertise.

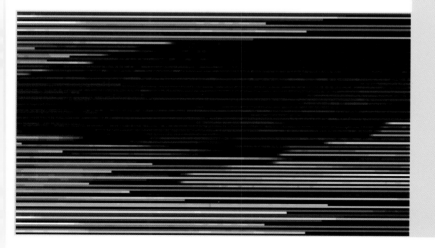

Funny Garbage

http://www.funnygarbage.com

New Yorker Peter Girardi's Web development studio proposes "making the Web worth watching" – and almost succeeds by not taking itself too seriously. Clients range from the Cartoon Network and NASCAR to Lego and the Experience Music Project.

Futurefarmers

http://www.futurefarmers.com

San Francisco-based multimedia maven Amy Franceschini founded this design collaborative "to explore the relationship of concept and creative process between interdisciplinary artists." Characterized by a quirky constellation of 3D modeling, spacey sound design and idiosyncratic content (including – full disclosure – a racy novella by this author), the site has long been a favorite destination of interactive design junkies.

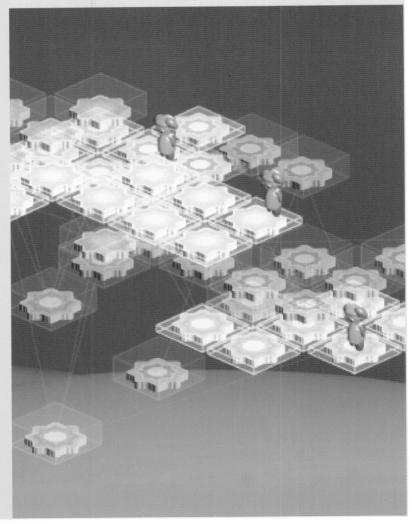

Jesse James Garrett

http://www.jjg.net

 G

This San Francisco-based designer hosts a personal "portal" with copious links to documents on information architecture and related subjects.

Giant Step

http://www.giantstep.com

Demonstrating admirable longevity in a cut-throat business climate, this Chicago-based consultancy wants you to know it's all about seriousness or, to use the site's media-speak, "strategic and creative solutions that leverage the medium's potential while maintaining the discipline of IT-based project management."

Milton Glaser Online

http://www.miltonglaser.com

The living icon of U.S. graphic design – who else has a more recognizable signature? – hawks signed copies of his famous posters (originals from his personal archives) from a site that describes his studio as "an interdisciplinary design office in business for a very long time."

Graphic Havoc

http://www.graphichavoc.com

A minimalist execution for this New York City-based multidisciplinary design group "specializing in unique solutions for international clients" features a handful of assignments for the Web and TV broadcast.

Green Lady

http://www.greenlady.com

Check out the devilishly clever template-motif implementation at this frankly promotional site for a T-shirt clothing designer.

Habitat 7

http://www.habitat7.de **H**

Forgoing the standard portfolio presentation, this self-promotion for WorX-online, a Zittau, Germany-based Web design studio, opts for a fictitious virtual tour. Don't be fooled by the muted palette, orthographic renderings, exquisite detailing, and dense annotation. This one's strictly for fun. The site also features links to other designers with far too much time on their hands.

John Hersey
http://www.hersey.com

Self-described as "one guy's advanced primate experiment," this diverting showcase for the talents of the wacky illustration whiz deploys visual wit and self-deprecating humor to present his eccentric graphic explorations. Hersey continuously reinvents the packaging, so check back early and often.

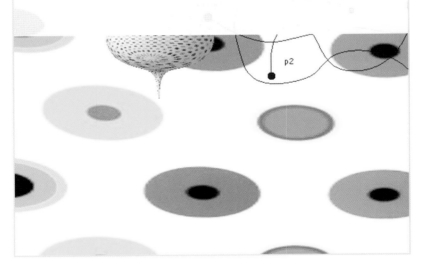

Hi-Res
http://www.hi-res.net

Few studio sites say "right now" as winningly as this portfolio for an up-and-coming British new-media outfit. The hyperactive creatives who once advertised the studio's slogan – "pixel pusher to the stars" – with an acid palette and ASCII-driven graphics replete with neo-constructivist lettering and orthographically rendered, animated "bots" have mellowed somewhat, and the promotion encompasses an impressive range of interactive projects, several of them for leading independent films.

Hillman Curtis
http://www.hillmancurtis.com

A canny self-promotion for the New York City-based motion graphics designer who advocates "making the invisible visible" features slickly conceived Web-based "mini-movies" created for a brace of top-drawer clients.

Hoefler Type Foundry
http://www.typography.com

Type designer Jonathan Hoefler and colleagues are known for the expressive yet controlled style of their typefaces, and perhaps best known for the Hoefler text family designed for Apple Computer and now part of the Macintosh operating system. The site posts work for the foundry's multifarious corporate and editorial clients, as well as a downloadable retail font collection that includes 13 exclusive type families with an esthetic firmly rooted in traditional and vernacular forms. A handy feature allows you to "test-drive" fonts before you buy them. There are also archives for *MUSE*, the studio's type specimen periodical.

Imaginary Forces
http://www.imaginaryforces.com

Movie-title design legend Kyle Cooper is perhaps best known for his incendiary credits for *Seven*, but that's history. Today he's running an industrial-strength studio working in film, broadcast, site, print and interactive design, presenting a spare but elegant portfolio that regrettably omits full-motion samples of the company's groundbreaking work.

Interaction Architect
http://www.interactionarchitect.com

Somewhat ungrammatically self-described as "a knowledge base on the human factor of interactive systems," such as corporate intranets, e-business and wireless applications, this online consultancy aims to encourage the development and exchange of interaction design expertise and professional methods, and support a professional identity for interaction architects.

Intro
http://www.introwebsite.com

An ingratiating, undulating abstract border frames the smoothly interactive wayfaring for this British studio, self-described as "part of the new-wave of innovative design and digital-media companies. Our eclectic mix of skills – design for print, design for digital media and design for moving image – positions us at the centre of the communications revolution."

K Kaliber 10000

http://www.k10k.dk

Now here's an anomaly: a goofy site devoted to mindless pleasures that's as pre-
cision-tooled as laser surgery – and as gracefully executed as the slickest agency
promo, only more so. Obsessively detailed by a couple of decidedly ungloomy
Danes, K10K ("The Designer's Lunch-box") revels in a miniscule scale that crams its
plethora of links, news and gossip, and silly interactive games into a portal-style
format. Hosts "mschmidt" and "toke" build their type and design on a pixel-based
module that,in less talented hands, would be downright excruciating to view. The
site posts weekly updates and has already accumulated a prodigious archive.

L Landor Associates

http://www.landor.com

The big, scarily entrenched San Francisco-based agency that just about invented modern corporate identity systems touts its Breakaway Brands™ (note
the trademark) and services.

Letterror

http://www.letterror.com

Type provocateurs with a distinguished track record, the creators of the
groundbreaking RandomFonts family host a "virtual office" that displays a vast
archive of brainy projects, doodles (animations drawn on a Palm Pilot are a
standout) and games, but also includes serious stuff like font showings, articles
and bibliographies.

Lineto

http://www.lineto.com

Founded by Cornel Windlin (in Zurich) and Stephan Mueller (in Berlin), this
loose-knit consultancy has designed digital typefaces based on environmental-
derived visual cues, from auto-registration plates,
public announcement display systems, and LCD
and dot matrix technologies, to output from
thermal printing and cargo-tagging devices.
A deliberately generic interface leads to
various departments that feature the duo's
strikingly contemporary type and design.

LinkDup
http://www.linkdup.com

Conscientiously maintained by Preloaded, a London-based new-media agency, this design portal enjoys good cred among Web cognoscenti for its firm grasp of aesthetics. Believing that what's "key to a good website is the ability to define your style," LinkDup – bucking the current Darwinian trend to cookie-cutter design – argues the case for expressiveness and visual delight. Every month the site's managers select their favorites from a continuous flow of submissions, filtering the winners into creative, promotional and resource categories. Their reviews are unabashedly non-professional, but sincere and to the point, and besides, there's always the hipness factor: this is one of the best places you can go to find the most far-out, up-to-the-minute Web design.

LiquidWit
http://www.liquidwit.com

Virtual brainstorming? What a concept! LiquidWit aims to field online creative teams that work together to come up with names, taglines, logo concepts, marketing ideas, and more. If it can find an audience, the service's ingenious and exhaustively detailed interface could stimulate or stifle the flow of ideas – it's hard to tell which. Either way the vividly articulated graphics are worth a look for their intelligent diagramming of the creative process. Failing that, LiquidWit – not an easy name to grasp or remember – could end up as yet another Web start-up with noble ambitions and a shaky business model.

LiveArea
http://www.livearea.com

Perhaps best-known for his award-winning site for OXO International, New York City-based founder Peter Comitini recently returned to home ground after a stint in the dot-com world. "Having a Web site challenges businesses to constantly re-evaluate the ways they express and build their relationships with the public," he says. "By balancing ideas and intuition in our interactive creative solutions, LiveArea turns information into understanding."

Lucidcircus
http://www.lucidcircus.com

As the International Space Station builds out in the background, an assaultive soundtrack dares you to continue. Inside, the site is quieter, more elegant, and a tricky but effective showcase for the Philadelphia-based studio's work for print, the Web, identity and the rest.

M

M.A.D.
http://www.madxs.com

Founders Erik Adigard and Patricia McShane drew attention with M.A.D.'s hyperkinetic Web site. Their recent redesign is radical in its simplicity while remaining experiential in nature. The entire site structure is anchored on the use of the scroll bar, an easily negotiable, one-window-for-all approach in which the global navigation repeats to form a ribbon down the full length of the site's single page.

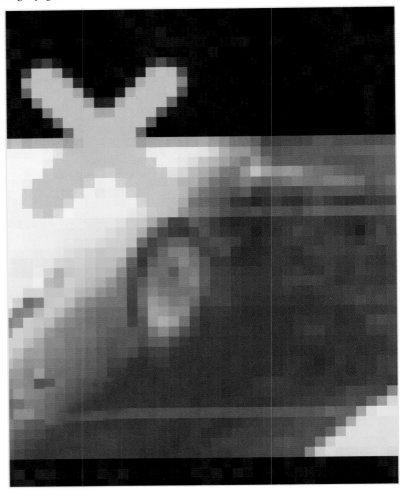

Bruce Mau
http://www.brucemaudesign.com

The dean of contemporary book design documents his ongoing collaboration with architects, publishers and cultural institutions with a spare execution for his Toronto studio that includes a plug for his backbreaking tome *Life Style*, "an incomplete manifesto for growth" which advances Mau's claim for the designer as author.

Me Company
http://www.mecompany.com

Sporting a vertiginous Op-Art graphic that literally sends you down the rabbit hole, this experimental interface launched to distribute desktop playthings and other goodies promotes a London-based design company "united by shared passions: modernity, technology, art and fashion."

Medium Rare
http://www.mediumrare.net

The London-based "old and new media design company" fields a cryptic interface for portfolio, declaring that "design is a contact sport" then, oddly enough, not showing any work.

MetaDesign
http://www.metadesign.com

Founded by type savant Erik Spiekermann, the designer of ingratiating and eminently serviceable fonts that are now well-nigh ubiquitous, this "international network of visual engineers" with offices in Berlin, San Francisco and Zurich provides a succinct introduction to its specialties: identity and branding, and interaction and information design.

Moccu

http://www.moccu.com

Jens Schmidt is the creative force behind The Secret Garden of Mutabor, the German agency's gorgeous, puzzling virtual playground. Working in tandem with a trio of designers, he recently launched a Web design and entertainment company whose presentation is just as strange and hermetic as his earlier project.

Modern Typography
http://www.moderntypography.com

Promising graphic design, typography, teaching, publishing, writing – what have they left out? – this crisply detailed destination was pre-launch when we last looked.

Colin Moock
http://www.moock.org

A nicely executed free-form resting-place for the author's thoughts on Web-related technology such as vector-based graphics, this one's being kept up-to-date. A companion site parades a couple of cute comic characters that involve some intriguing cursor play.

Morla Design
http://www.morladesign.com

San Francisco-based graphic-design doyen Jennifer Morla presents a pleasantly decorated portfolio with an interactive component conceived as a formalist exercise and described as "an experiment ... that explores the nature of communication through Internet dialogue."

Mutabor
http://www.mutabor.com

This self-promotion for a Hamburg-based studio blends work-for-hire and ordering information for the firm's bilingual magazine with an eccentric "playground" dubbed The Secret Garden of Mutabor. Behind a drop-dead gorgeous interface, the brazenly style-conscious site musters impressive programming tricks that transmute the studio's corporate identity into quirky animations. The result is a kinetic experience that's outstanding for its lush, earth-toned palette, gauzy atmospheric effects and subtle auditory cues. The navigation of Mutabor ("I'm going to change") constantly toys with your expectations, goading and rewarding you with half-buried clues. It doesn't all work, of course. Vital contact information is set in tiny, indecipherable type, and only the most diligent visitors will negotiate the Secret Garden's perversely complex maze of commands.

Nofrontiere
http://www.nofrontiere.com

Merry pranksters when the mood strikes them, this Vienna-based consultancy visually articulates its structure as a series of blobs – a system of "virtual operating units" that overlap to form a floating system "linked by common goals and interests in the international context of the design world."

Nomex
http://www.nomex.net

This Montreal-based consultancy offers three tiers of services: Web marketing, solutions development and electronic marketing. Sporting a distinctly individual visual intelligence, Nomex isn't cut from the usual technocentric cloth.

Norm
http://www.norm.to

Zurich-based designers Dimitri Bruni and Manuel Krebs have crafted a Web version of minimalist sculpture with this terse display for their 2-D and 3-D projects, page layouts from their eponymous book and links to a couple of exemplary font showings.

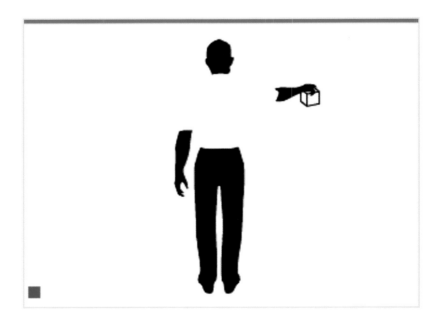

One9ine
http://www.one9ine.com

According to designers Warren Corbitt and Matt Owen, "creative work should have an energy and freshness of approach that makes the client, audience and designer excited and engaged." A small but substantial portfolio bears out their proof-of-process.

Orange Juice Design
http://www.i-jusi.com

We can't wait to see what this Durban-based design collective – publishers of *i-jusi*, an incendiary broadside magazine that plays fast and loose with the South African visual vernacular – have in store for us at their Web destination. When we last looked it was still pre-launch, but the creators are promising cover art, collaborations and free stuff.

The Orphanage
http://www.theorphanage.com

Founded by a group of former Industrial Light & Magic visual-effects artists, this San Francisco-based "next-wave" production company, dedicated to producing innovative digital entertainment for theatrical release, posts several downloadable short films and information on its groundbreaking proprietary technology.

Parisfrance
http://www.parisfranceinc.com

With the slogan "we invent places where people love to go," this Portland, Oregon-based Web design consultancy shows off a sophisticated treatment for its small but select clientele, along with weekly postings on the studio's activities. An intriguing section titled "The Machines of Joy" grapples in poster form with interactive design issues.

Pentagram
http://www.pentagram.com

Long a fixture on the international design scene, the huge but well-respected agency posts a scrolling supergraphic that points to a staggering array of assignments including editorial, identity, branding and interactive design.

Pixel Brothers
http://www.pixelbrothers.co.uk

A London-based studio that creates interactive media and programming, posts online games that exhibit varying degrees of design ingenuity.

PRACTICE

Pixel Surgeon
http://www.pixelsurgeon.com

Designer Jason Arber hosts a busy meeting place for interviews, articles and reviews that hawks type fonts while posting plentiful links to the cyberhip-oisie.

Plumb
http://www.plumbdesign.com

This New York City-based consultancy is perhaps best known for its Thinkmap software, a remarkable information technology, based on visually representing data relationships, that "lets organizations share complex information through interfaces that transform facts and data into insight and knowledge."

Post Tool
http://www.posttool.com

San Francisco-based founders David Karam and Gigi Obrecht have successfully juggled personal projects with work-for-hire, producing a remarkably varied range of commissions for print and electronic media that test the line between art and design. Fundamental to their purpose is guiding the reader/viewer. "If the last millennium was concerned with the pursuit of information, the coming millennium will surely be taken up with the task of making our way through the mass of data we have accumulated," Obrecht writes. "The greatest challenge of the information age is not discovery but navigation. The world of new media needs guides and mapmakers, and our ambition is to contribute to this effort."

Quickface
http://www.quickface.com

Q

Manhattan Beach, California-based designers and developers Bryan Dorsey and Mateo Neri have created collaborative enterprise software that improves process, time efficiency and scalability, to substantially reduce the cost of Web development. By providing structure and organization to the process, the package allows for the efficient use of tools, applications and people across the enterprise. The designers claim the software eliminates three "massive" corporate Web site development problems, streamlining the process, providing a common architecture, and bundling resource management tools.

QuickHoney
http://www.quickhoney.com

New York-based ex-Berliners Nana Rausch and Peter Stemmler promote their illustration from this vaguely disquieting site. Click on one of the beehives on the splash page and you're sent to Rausch's Soap-Machine, a downbeat study of domestic malaise. Or view Stemmler's extensive portfolio of magazine work, uncannily similar in style to his partner's. Enter Rausch's "Our Small World," and you're escorted through a 32-panel, text-free, semi-autobiographical "novella" that chronicles those mundane routines – eating, screwing, watching TV, riding the subway – that constitute their lives. Stemmler's work focuses on the figure, while Rausch's deadpan renderings leach all the texture out of their urban settings, leaving as their residue an outsider's take on the familiar urban milieu. Don't miss the sushi-tray assembly line.

85

Razorfish

http://www.razorfish.com

Poster boys for the integration of design and technology on the Internet, New York City-based founders Jeff Dachis and Craig Kanarek have expanded their activities voraciously over the years. With offices now in 15 major cities world-wide, you'd think these Silicon Alley denizens risked diluting their offer, but the Razorfish juggernaut – despite the occasional setback – shows no sign of letting up.

Reala

http://www.reala.se

The work of Stockholm-based illustrators Samuel Nyholm and Jonas Williamson exists in a cartoonish, vaguely malevolent world distinct from the clarity and severity of traditional Scandinavian design. Concocting bizarrely rendered "sign-families" composed of figures, fonts and pictograms that populate their short online animations, the duo have developed a mutating symbolism that comes to life as a "tribe" of signs.

ReThink Paper

http://www.rethinkpaper.org

Sponsored by the eco-activist Earth Island Institute, this well-executed site promotes non-wood solutions for print, with the reminder that there will never be enough wood fiber to supply the ever-growing appetite of the global pulp and paper industry. A handy paper selector introduces you to suppliers of op-tional sources, from banana stalks, coffee-bean residue and industrial hemp to tobacco, sugarcane and cotton waste. You'll have to look elsewhere, how-ever, for basic information on materials such as kenaf, a field crop indigenous to West Africa that is considered one of the most promising alternatives to virgin soft and hard woods.

R/GA Digital Design

http://www.rga.com

Pioneers in the field of computerized motion graphics, New York City-based R/GA has over the years been associated with many of the classics of the motion-picture title genre and later advancements in the field of interactive design – on which the studio now focuses exclusively.

Saatchi & Saatchi
http://www.saatchi.be

Self-described, with admirable restraint, as "the hottest ideas shop on the planet," the Belgian advertising behemoth was reportedly slow to rise to the challenge of interactive online communications. A stylish self-promotion replete with bells and whistles fosters the breathtaking insight that "ideas are the currency of the future."

Sapient
http://www.sapient.com

With a grand total of 20 offices (all but two of them in the U.S.), Sapient – promising "The right team. The right technology. The right results" – has held on to a reputation for well-thought-out design in a chilly business climate for large consultancies.

Second Story
http://www.secondstory.com

Portland, Oregon-based interactive designers Julie Beeler and Brad Johnson have achieved an enviable track record for editorial-based work and for researching and developing original content for major educational TV network programming. On their site, which includes an eye-catching panoramic virtual tour, they state that "The studio's eclectic team of creative artists, producers, writers, animators, and programmers is dedicated to educating, entertaining and inspiring audiences through storytelling innovation."

J. otto Seibold
http://www.jotto.com

Children's book favorite J. otto advertises his talents with a playful self-promotion that effectively deploys a series of Flash animations populated by loopy characters bordering on the surreal.

Siegelgale
http://www.siegelgale.com

Offering "ideas that transform," this U.S.-based consultancy – the site's vague about office locations – promotes its longstanding experience with solving complex communications problems through e-business strategy and brand development.

Signalgrau
http://www.signalgrau.com

The site for Dirk Uhlenbrock's Essen-based studio is a terse iteration that's mostly in German but posts news in English of recent accounts.

Slo Graffiti
http://www.slograffiti.com

An innovative Los Angeles-based multimedia development company that postulates the cross-breeding of film direction, design and other disciplines, this fledgling outfit already boasts alignments with a prestigious roster of indie talent.

Smashing Type
http://www.smashingtype.com

Conceived "to bring together typographers and lettering artists with designers, students and everyday desktop publishers to celebrate letters in all forms," and published by Dreadnaught, a Toronto type house, Smashing Type is well on its way to delivering some substantial content. There's also a better-than-average online art gallery and, among other contemporary work, photographs of tasteful underwater nudes forming the letters of the alphabet.

State
http://www.statedesign.com

Another deft exploration of the tactile potential of interactive interfaces by a London-based cross-media consultancy. Instead of visually depicting the studio's portfolio, the site opts for a stylized representation of the work, with links elsewhere to the actual material.

Stating the Obvious
http://www.theobvious.com

Web maven Michael Sippey dispenses advice through this opinionated columns post that frequently deals with interactive and information design issues.

Sticky Ideas
http://www.stickyideas.com

Ungrammatically self-described as "the online resource to read expert advice from creative folks who have been in the trenches," this bustling destination also points to Web sites and books that "will get [sic] your creative spark lit ..."

Studio AKA

http://www.studioaka.co.uk

A no-frills interface displays an impressive range of un-hackneyed illustration styles from a London-based consortium of half-a-dozen animators and interactive designers.

91

Studio Dumbar

http://www.studiodumbar.com

The legendary Dutch graphic-design shop has registered its url, but the site was mysteriously blank whenever we looked.

Surface

http://www.surface.de

Frankfurt-based founders Markus Weisbeck and Andreas Vitt maintain a design studio focused on corporate and institutional design, "especially when a unified design concept is needed that crosses different media – old and new." An imposing portfolio displays an astonishing range of work, from installations and album covers to posters and logos.

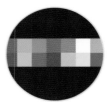

T-26

http://www.t26.com

The Chicago-based digital type foundry headed by designer Carlos Segura boasts 500 typeface families with a cybernetic flavor from 200 designers worldwide. A "zoom-in feature" lets you get up close and personal.

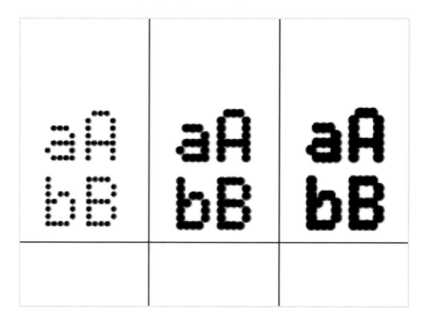

Theory into Practice
http://www.uvm.edu/~jrc/workshop

The University of Vermont posts a tutorial, "Using Information Theory to Evaluate Your Website," that includes exercises, design guides and sections on information design guru Edward Tufte, information problem-solving and technology.

They Might Be Giants
http://www.tmbg.com

The quirky music group posts a bizarrely inventive splash page that's reminiscent of a circus sideshow's shooting gallery. Take aim at the targets to hear some tantalizingly brief audio samples.

Thirst
http://www.3st.com

Chicago-based design gadfly Rick Valicenti's forum for sounding off on such vital issues as e-mail orthography and showings of the Thirstype collection. The edgy editorial content is way out of date, but the studio's 20-font typeface family holds its own.

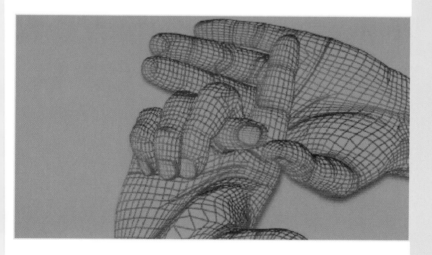

Thousand Words
http://www.thousand-words.com

A New York City-based film production and finance company associated with some of the indie movement's groundbreaking hits provides a section devoted to articles, tips and links of interest to aspiring filmmakers.

Tolleson Design

http://www.tolleson.com

Opening with a seductive informational tease, the site for this San Francisco-based studio renowned for its masterful typographic execution was awaiting launch when we looked.

Tomato

http://www.tomato.co.uk

Now in its second decade of operation, the much-acclaimed British multimedia studio has influenced a generation of discourse on electronic design. In recent years, films and interactive design for CD-ROMs have formed a large part of the legacy, and the site complies with a mini-gallery of Shockwave experiments.

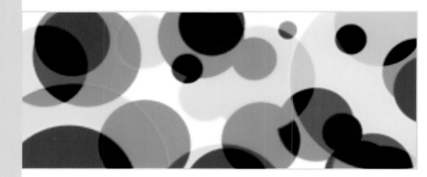

Trollbäck & Co.

http://www.trollback.com

Worth a visit for its bold graphics alone, this self-promotion for a New York City-based motion-graphics house, staffed mainly by young European designers, employs an ingenious elevator motif as an armature for a portfolio that includes a highly watchable virtual "reel."

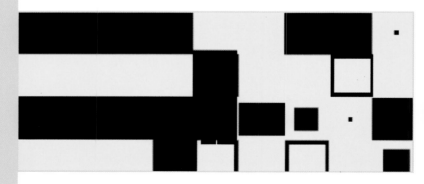

Turner Duckworth Design
http://www.turnerduckworth.com

The London- and San Francisco-based consultancy that finesses "leading consumer brands in changing categories" posts a boldly silhouetted graphic which gets the bi-continental message across.

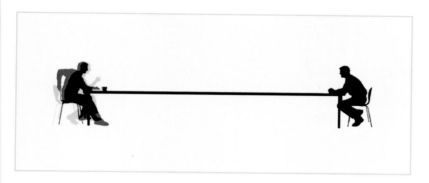

Twenty2product
http://www.twenty2.com

This San Francisco-based agency specializing in interactive design and motion graphics posts generous samplings of an impressive range of assignments.

Twothousandstrong
http://www.2000strong.com

The Venice, California-based motion graphics studio effectively promotes an output ranging from film, editorial, and 3D and 2D animation, to sound design, typography, special effects and logo design.

Typebox
http://www.typebox.com

Based in the San Francisco Bay Area, graphic designers Mike Kohnke and Joachim Müller-Lancé collaborate on this online font shop-cum-design quarterly that promotes type culture. Addressing a small, but increasingly influential coterie, the fledgling site's seasonal updates look slight but promising. Typebox offers content ranging from insider design tips (a discussion of the proper vertical positioning of m-dashes) to a lively overview of the tight-knit, and frequently just plain quirky, international typographic scene. Font showings by the founders, as well as invited designers, are imbued with a retro-futuristic-inflected contemporary feel.

Typotheque
http://www.typotheque.com

Exotically based in Bratislava, Slovakia, graphic design whiz Peter Bilak's Internet-based independent type foundry offers fonts, proprietary type utilities, articles on the subject, and tips for using and creating fonts, as well as a short list of hard-to-find books you can order on graphic design and typography.

Uiweb
http://www.uiweb.com

Should you trust Microsoft's authority on UI design and usability? You wouldn't think so, but Scott Berkun's writings on web and interaction design, archived here, flesh out the issues of using critical thinking to generate and manage good ideas in design.

Use It
http://www.useit.com

Usability guru Jakob Nielsen's virtually graphics-free discussion of "usable information technology" features an Alertbox archiving advice – still anathema to many Web designers – that champions the user experience as a priority. Agree or disagree, Nielsen's prescriptions for Web viability merit discussion.

VBureau
http://www.vbureau.com

V

Announcing a virtual incarnation of the sociopolitically-conscious New York City-based studio headed by Marlene McCarthy that was once "part of the corporeal world," a terse iteration leaves you guessing – and guessing.

Vignelli Associates NY
http://www.vignelli.com

According to its underplayed, bells-and-whistles-free site, echt-modernist Massimo Vignelli's New York City-based firm "has set the standard for total design by providing for an international clientele a complete range of services, including the design of graphic and corporate identity programs, publications, environmental graphics, exhibitions and interiors, furniture and consumer products." He needs to learn a few new tricks. When we looked, sloppy linking led to several dead ends.

Web Page Design for Designers
http://www.wpdfd.com

W

Technically a zine, since it posts monthly updates, the site is devoted to practice in terms of the "creative side" of Web design – graphics, typography, writing – and "free-thinking."

Webmonkey
http://hotwired.lycos.com/webmonkey

Hotwired's web developer section presents hip but no-nonsense advice from certified geek freaks on a spectrum of design and technology issues, helpfully arranged into Beginner, Builder and Master categories.

WM Team
http://www.wmteam.de

So that's how it's done. The rib-tickling promotion for a Hanover, Germany-based advertising consultancy furnishes what has to be the last word on how concepts get designed with technology. Hint: follow the compactor model (you'll see).

Writers Block
http://www.baresquare.com/play/writersblock

A special section of this rambling blog features a step-by-step walk through of just about every Web design cliché you can think of – and a few you probably haven't.

Xplane
http://www.xplane.com

X

Considering all the hoopla about information design, there's a dearth of knowledgeable commentary on the subject both online and off. St. Louis-based Xplane, a small, young studio with an established track record for creating fresh and communicative information graphics, works to remedy the situation. The firm specializes in a vivid, cartoon-like house style intended to unravel the complex realities of hi-tech companies – and they take this stuff seriously. Their site hosts an online posting of links to relevant and informative articles that is updated almost daily. Topics covered in the studio's "visual thinking web log" and case studies include GUIs, cartographic maps and discussions of internet protocols and brand strategy.

Yale University Style Guide
http://info.med.yale.edu/caim/manual/interface/navigation.html

Y

Yale's manual for interface design for the Web reminds us that "users of Web documents don't just look at information, they interact with it in novel ways that have no precedents in paper document design." Furthermore, "Graphic design and visual 'signature' graphics are not just used to 'jazz up' Web pages. Graphics are an integral part of the user's experience with your site. In interactive documents it is impossible to fully separate graphic design from issues of interface design."

PRACTICE ■

PROJECTS

A group of designers who pool whimsical and self-indulgent doodles in a kinetic free-for-all that tests your concentration skills. An animator who posts progress reports on his Web site about his ongoing film project. A writer who has learned to integrate words with pictures and sound to create an eerie, otherworldly viewing experience. Scattered across the vastness of the Web, projects by a plethora of creative talents demonstrate the seemingly infinite willingness of humans to befuddle, charm and amaze each other.

From its very beginnings, the Web has provided a playground for design with little or no commercial or business value. Spilling out of earlier multimedia work for CD-ROM, online projects have evolved along with successive generations of technological break-throughs that build on the Web's ability to synthesize audio and visual elements with an economy never before possible. The ease of collaboration the Web engenders has led to an unprecedented cross-fertilization of ideas for transmuting design into unforeseen new forms and feelings.

An unregulated marketplace of ideas, the Web gives shape and color to uncensored, sometimes even transgressive, modes of expression. In its immediacy, it provides a home for the very latest design trends, and the relentless pace of experiment it encourages has accelerated as artists of all kinds are instantly updated on each other's work.

Alt77

http://www.alt77.com

A cryptic birthday greeting to a fictional subject identified solely by a serial number marked this minimalist aural-and-visual experiment on a recent visit.

Babel

http://www.babel.uk.net

Australian artist Simon Biggs hearkens back to the Dewey Decimal System in this collective interactive work. Organized as a series of square grids that form a cube consisting of rows of numbers floating in space, the piece responds to the cumulative movements of groups of visitors whose interactions collide in random, colored explosions.

Bits and Pieces

http://www.noodlebox.com/bitsandpieces

Some years ago, Liverpool native Daniel Brown began posting sound-and-motion studies with unusual metaphors for interaction that featured ethereal animations. His new subsite's dozen or so separate exercises are distinguished by dreamy textures and intriguing implementation of plug-ins to form new variations on shape and texture.

Bulbo

http://www.bulbo.com

Mishmash Media's Seth Feinberg has a reputation for off-key animation on the Web, but the irrepressible Bulbo, his personal creation, is stranger by far than all the rest. To the accompaniment of a vintage movie orchestra, Bulbo – rendered in a deranged version of classic animation style – encounters a series of adventures from which, thanks to his, er, unusual anatomy, he always emerges unscathed. Check out the episode that takes him through a 100-year timeline of modern history.

Chroma
http://www.marrowmonkey.com/chroma

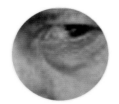

An interactive sci-fi novella by multimedia artist
Erik Loyer is a special feature at his "Lair of
the Marrow Monkey." Loyer has concocted an
eerily convincing tale in 1 6 installments that
are designed to manipulate readers' perceptions
depending on how they interact with the
material. An exquisitely realized, Lego-inspired
interface significantly improves the experience.

Combine
http://www.combine.org

With the warning that "now is a good time to start worrying," this playful but
disturbing promotion features off-beat collaborations from designers George
Larou and Andy Slopsema. A trippy interface introduces a hard-to-read display
that's consistent with the gnomic character of the imagery.

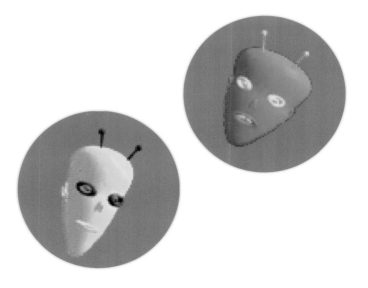

Shane Cooper
http://www.shanecooper.com

A New Zealand artist posts a series of interactive experiments involving text and
voice. One such warns that "anything you type will be spoken in the room you
see by a voice synthesizer connected to a powerful speaker system, so be careful
of your spelling."

Dept
http://www.dept.nl

The virtual playground for Amsterdam-based designer Don Leo's Machine studio bristles with in-your-face motion graphics and interactive games. If you're the nervous type, you may want to avoid the apparently fictional virus "RSI 2000."

Design Garten
http://www.designgarten.com

Hailing from Germany, this grab-bag of a site composes itself around roughly a score of bite-size doodles, jokey animations and the like.

Digital Experiences
http://www.digital-experiences.com

Enter this virtual playroom created by London-based multimedia firm Digit, Inc. and, once you get the hang of its low-key but ingenious interface, you're in for some mindlessly amusing, screensaver-style type-and-motion experiments. The site also has links to a handful of other kindred design spirits and to Digit's commercial portfolio.

E eBoy

http://www.eboy.com

Think of it as a dystopian version of *Sim City*, the enormously popular make-
believe-scenario computer game that positions you as the mover-and-shaker
in a fungible, but ultimately controllable world. eBoy's Sim-like, orthographically
rendered mindscapes don't have the original game's interactivity, but they are
a sobering reflection of their creators' anxieties. The perpetrators, eBoy partners
Steffen Sauerteig, Kai Vermehr, Svend Smital and Peter Stemmler, sell their
eponymous font family – based on the geometry of pixeled screen fonts and
created specially for use onscreen and on the Web – via the site.

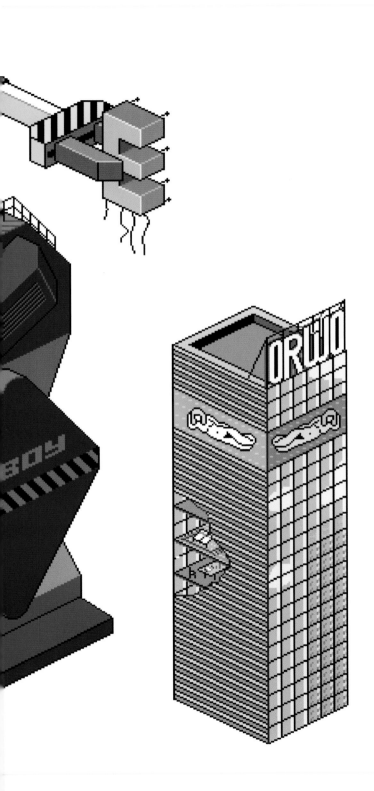

Etoy

http://etoy.com

The Swiss-based conceptualists-turned-corporate-gadflies that terrorized dot-com casualty Etoys some years ago host a cryptic fan site replete with the latest party and meeting photos.

EverQuest

http://everquest.station.sony.com

It's a grim place, the PC-based graphic-user-interface environment. A calculated online clone of *Ultima*, the inexplicably popular medieval fantasy game, *EverQuest* perpetuates the original's aesthetically challenged virtual world. An enormous "place," it's a mutable setting for players to equip themselves for a variety of cheesy adventures. But the game replaces *Ultima*'s grimly orthographic rendering with an approximation of 3D that's at least consistent with its characters and situations.

Extrabad

http://www.extrabad.com

A cubistic break-dancing animation – and that's it.

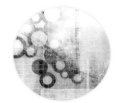

Factory 512

http://factory512.com

Its original mission to foster "kick-ass inspirations and fuck-brains [sic] projects," this former e-zine has been retooled by creator Dmitry Utkin as a hub that posts a gallery of links to splashy graphics experiments.

Flazoom

http://www.flazoom.com

A fan site for projects that implement the now well-nigh ubiquitous Flash plug-in posts blurbs about the latest outstanding applications and archives a library of links to other worthy specimens.

Force Feed: Swede
http://forcefeedswede.com

To the sound of a vaguely nautical ambient sound-track, designer Oz Dean posts sporadic design news and links to friends at a transitional destination that's as ingratiating as many more fully-realized sites.

Half Empty
http://www.halfempty.com

 H

Besides a grab-bag of art-related articles by host Marty Spellerberg and a handful of other contributors, the home of this highly idiosyncratic collective is notable for the "Blink Playbin," a blog for unsolicited Flash and Shockwave experiments that seems to stretch to infinity.

Heavy
http://www.heavy.com

Comedy is hard. Cheap cynicism ("Behind the Music That Sucks") is easy. The pricey subscription service at this music-oriented site hosted by a New York City-based multimedia firm redeems itself with in-your-face graphics, but the mockumentary approach definitely has its limits. Non-members are subjected to excruciatingly long advertising downloads.

Honest
http://www.stayhonest.com

A morphing Rorshach blot sets the tone for this strangely involving site. Ostensibly a promotion for the New York City-based "multidisciplinary" design firm of the same name, the ongoing project ambitiously "explores what it means to be honest and a designer, and the inherent contradictions when you try to be both." With its loopy graphics and "polygraph tests," it's more like a free-for-all virtual sandbox of experimentation by many and varied talents than a straight portfolio.

IngredientX
http://www.ingredientx.com

New York City-based "videographers" Emre and Lev Yilmaz (brothers, we presume) have combined their animation and puppet-making skills to produce a slew of clever short subjects, archived here for your indulgence. Don't miss "The Hurt Inner Child Show."

Introversion
http://www.introversion.com

Posting "daily episodes from my life," San Francisco-based multimedia artist Patrick Kalvanapu elevates navel-gazing to an art form with pop-up diaristic jottings rendered in a faux-techno interface.

Jodi
http://www.jodi.org

Long before the Web itself became consumed with self-doubt, enigmatic code-as-art made this stunning but chilly site the granddaddy of online deconstruction.

Just in Space
http://www.justinspace.com

A self-styled "concept designer" for themed environments and interactive displays posts trashy and enthusiastic contributions to kitsch culture along with his portfolio. Check out the highly unauthorized Ebay Conceptual Art Gallery, and a series of "Obscene Interiors" that critiques the decorating skills of amateur porn stars.

Kraftwerk
http://www.kraftwerk.com

Yielding none of its secrets to the casual visitor, the virtual home to Germany's graying techno-music avatars makes a dubious virtue of minimalism.

LaPuCo
http://www.lapuco.com

LaPuCo is an online multi-player environment that aims to extend multi-player interaction beyond simple chat rooms and message boards without requiring users to commit to the medieval or sci-fi mythologies of most multi-player games. Set on a lush but monochromatic island indigenously populated with little square people, the game invites players to become "squares" themselves. By finding and playing mini-games scattered throughout the island, players can develop their squares and imbue them with special skills and abilities. Players can also interact with one another by chatting and trading, encouraging the development of a diverse population and a simple economy. As more economic opportunities present themselves, more opportunities for exploration are revealed.

Lust
http://www.lust.nl

Advertising "Typography, Design & Propaganda," but apparently dormant, this showcase for a Dutch graphic design studio based in The Hague, Netherlands, is still a benchmark of bold and innovative interface design that includes a striking, if somewhat dated, font portfolio. The creators espouse a design philosophy that "revolves around coincidence, the degradation of form and content to essence, and contextuality versus textuality."

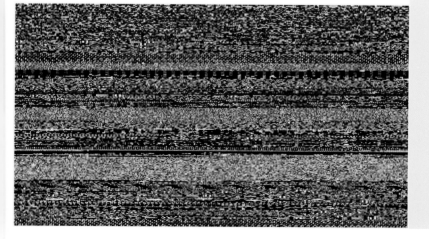

Mariot Hotel
http://www.themariothotel.com

Technically an online zine, "the ultrafashion
porn magazine" offers a curious mix of couture,
art and sex geared to – so help us – the
creative community.

Mobiles Disco
http://www.mobilesdisco.com

Audio loops can get old really fast, but the infectious sound track on the splash
page for the Mobiles – a wacky Finnish hip-hop group – worms its way into your
ear. After a leisurely download, some devilishly clever code ushers you inside a
virtual bistro where your customized stand-in can dance and mingle, and a comely,
Finnish-speaking "barlady" takes your drink orders (but good luck getting her
attention). Surprise, you've stumbled into one of those "chat worlds" where visitors exchange e-mail banalities in a virtual environment. Most are grim, artlessly
rendered places, but this one has a hipster ambience that attracts patrons who
can carry on an informed discussion around, say, the latest techno hip-hop
recordings. Don't forget to visit the charming downstairs dance floor, with its
rotating disco ball.

Mr Blowup
http://www.mrblowup.com

This, um, highly personal site records what can be viewed as an ongoing
performance piece by a British devotee of the inflatable lifestyle.

Myst III
http://www.myst3.com

The creators of the original *Myst* – the fantasy adventure game which captivated
legions of fans during the period of the CD-ROM format's now-faded popularity –
have since departed the project. Their successors have produced a sequel that
retains the magic realism of the core game and captures its uncanny evocation of
a fictional but oddly convincing world. While enhancing interactivity and easing
navigation, the new version preserves the original game's static and sometimes
impenetrable presentation, and *Myst* persists as something of an artifact from an
earlier, less sophisticated era of gaming.

Net Baby World
http://www.netbabyworld.com

Giving crass commercialism a post-ironic spin, this Swedish purveyor of multi-player online games allows you to play for free. Consistent with their belief that taking part in any of the activities should be nothing but fun, "no product from Netbabyworld contains lethal violence or sexual elements." Instead, the characters and situations are jokey, infantile and stylish, and there's an "eco-house" you can build brick by brick.

Once Upon a Forest
http://www.once-upon-a-forest.com

O

To a scratchy ambient score, PrayStation's creator (see next entry) posts a gallery of some 30 motion graphics experiments. Most have a shard-like quality that is uninvolving, but there are several free-form exercises that flirt with an elusive visual appeal.

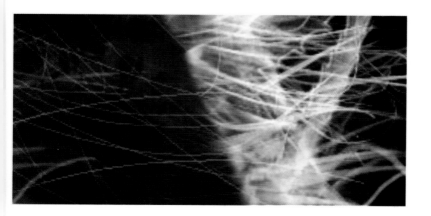

P

PrayStation
http://www.praystation.com

This long-time favorite of interactive display cognoscenti features Single Cell, a monthly "bestiary" of new Web life forms. Creator Joshua Davis deploys a scrolling wall-calendar format that nicely maps the project's peaks of activity.

Presstube
http://www.presstube.com

The folks at Design Is Kinky post mural-like renderings that have a chaotic quality at this deliberately off-putting site.

R

Rockstar Games
http://www.rockstargames.com

In an odd amalgam of corporate hucksterism and cutting-edge graphics, you stumble on links to curiosities like a do-it-yourself rap recording.

RPSONC
http://ameba.lpt.fi/~tsuviala/rpsonc.html

This Finnish entry features the rib-tickling antics of Rabbi Phunkiewsky's School of New Communication, an interactive virtual boom-box that you play like a musical keyboard, to hilarious effect.

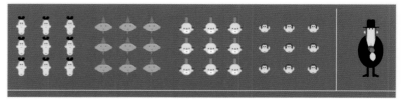

RSUB Network

http://www.rsub.com

Once a stimulating destination, before parent company Razorfish became
synonymous with the big, bad and ugly, this former home for cutting-edge Web
experimentation is now a display case for several disquieting animations
mainly distinguished for their gross-out misogynist humor.

®™mark

http://www.rtmark.com

A conceptual art project masquerading as "corporate consulting for the 21st
century," ®™mark posts such curiosities as electronic greeting cards for capital
punishment. In the hands of these art-world
subversives, "limited liability" is an artistic strategy
that supports the sabotage of corporate products –
from dolls and children's learning tools to
electronic action games – by channeling funds
from investors to workers for specific projects
grouped into categories of "mutual funds."

Rustboy

http://www.rustboy.com

Creator Brian Taylor documents his work in process, a years-in-the-making online animated film using "modest, affordable" home software without the benefit
of high-end 3D packages usually associated with this sort of filmmaking (if that's
what we're still calling it). Although unfinished, *Rustboy* is already riveting, as
shown by the mini-movies Taylor posts along with diaries, concept art and story-
boards that document his decision-making and explore his artistic strategies.

Screenshots
http://www.whitelead.com/jrh/screenshots

Artist Jon Haddock has amassed an unnerving body of work which includes a series of depictions of historic settings – like the underground garage where Lee Harvey Oswald was shot – that he digitally altered to eliminate their human subjects. With "Screenshots," the Tempe, Arizona-based provocateur reverses the process, exploring the role of human representation in a series of true or imagined gritty urban dramas. Rendered in isometric perspective and reminiscent of computer games, Haddock's eerily wooden recreations of such real-life events as the assassination of Martin Luther King are displayed interchangeably with fictional scenes like the jury-room confrontation in the film *Twelve Angry Men*.

The Sex Slave Decalogue
http://www.goultralightsgo.com/naoki/decalogue/decalogue.html

Los Angeles-based artist Naoki Mitsuse's crisply delineated animations have the look of paper cutouts that borrow from the iconography of fetishism and, um, scuba diving and other sources. In the protracted 10-part saga's ultimate sequence, the series' eponymous anti-hero mixes it up with fighter pilots and gets the best of a sinister, gun-wielding TV monitor.

Shorn
http://www.shorn.com

Promising "entertainment for the ill-tempered" this stubbornly eccentric destination – still in prototype when we looked – appears to have commercial ambitions. Shorn's less-than-hirsute host introduces a raft of situational games (hellish dating scenarios are a persistent motif) framed by so-1990s deconstructivist graphics that are spiked with oddball audio cues. A nice touch at the welcome, it lets you select a soundtrack: choose from ambient, trip-hop, drum 'n' bass or best of all, no sound (it's only the rare audio loop that doesn't get tired really fast). Wiseass, cynical, manipulative – what's not to like?

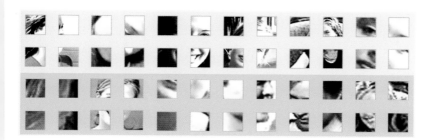

16 Color
http://www.16color.com

Every week host Alan Watts posts crude but effective mini-animations from guest artists on "The Internet Movie Machine."

Soul Bath
http://www.soulbath.com

At a well-favored site that playfully deconstructs the Web's much-vaunted interactivity, the designers delight in frustrating users' expectations, at a keystroke unleashing torrents of ASCII-based gibberish and taunting "instructions." On a recent visit, the site was posting "Click Here," an exhibition of "anti-banners."

Stamen
http://www.stamen.com

San Francisco-based designer Eric Rodenbeck keeps a voluminous diary at this personal site. In relaunch mode when we visited, it provides an unfiltered view of life in the trenches of the city's Multimedia Gulch.

Super Bad
http://www.superbad.com

A cheerfully minimalist setting for an erratic display that intermittently posts games and graphics.

Tech Flesh

http://ctheorymultimedia.cornell.edu

Curated by Ctheory, a group of radical academics with a marked semiotics-oriented bent, this multimedia presentation on the topic of "the problems and perils of the human genome project" contains artistic works relating to "transgenic flesh," "sequential tracings" and "recombinant cells."

They Rule

http://theyrule.orgo.org

It's no news that consolidation of power among the world corporate and government elites continues at a breakneck pace. What has been missing is a clear explanation of how they're all interconnected. New Zealander Josh On has performed the daunting task of consolidating information on the U.S. ruling class – later to build out to a dissection of enclaves worldwide – into an on-line display that cogently expresses the incestuous ties that bind our multinational movers-and-shakers. Using the Flash plug-in, On has crafted a simple, intuitive interface that allows visitors to explore this intricate and secretive web of complicity. The ingeniously conceived site marries intelligent information design to a radical, even subversive, political agenda.

Thru the Moebius Strip

http://www.moebius-strip.com

Frustrating dead-ends mar the navigation on this promotional site for *Tron* creator Jean "Moebius" Giraud's fully computer animated feature-film-in-the-works, but offer tantalizing glimpses of the long-awaited project's ravishing visuals. A curious feature: downloadable "paper cuts" you print out and assemble to construct examples of Giraud's 3D artworks.

Tint

http://www.tint.de

A German-based interface designer posts an inventive array of typefaces (including Binary, "the smallest screen-optimized font the universe has ever seen"), Shockwave games, and an assortment of snapshots and personal observations.

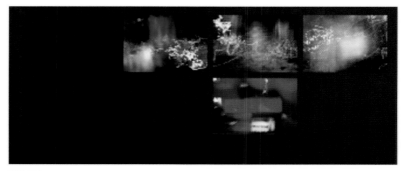

Trans
http://www.transmag.org

This ongoing Web project is hosted by architect Hani Rashid and launched to lead to the eventual completion in book form of a text devoted to arts, culture and media. The "telesymposium" attracts some of the best and brightest talents in the design world – then rewards them with an all-but-unreadable interface for presenting their remarks.

Turbulence
http://www.turbulence.org

For the last half-decade, this cultural resource has commissioned and supported about twenty Internet art projects annually, most by New York City-based artists. The site boasts an exhaustive archive and monthly installments of SINGLECELL, an "online bestiary" made up of "a collection of interactive life-forms discovered and reared by a diverse group of computational artists and designers."

Turux
http://www.turux.org

Mysterious German illustrators "Lia" and "Dextro" post a gallery of largely mono-chromatic formalist exercises that have their own weird beauty. What little text is displayed in English is full of noncommittal allusions to recreational drugs.

Typographic 56
http://www.typographic56.co.uk

An ambitious group effort to present a score of discrete "explorations into [sic] onscreen typography," this experimental forum, developed by London-based new-media agency Deepend, inadvertently raises some troubling issues regarding de-signers and their relationship to content and text. Visually arresting as the exhibits are, their impact is consistently undermined by typo-strewn, ungrammatical text (presumably written by the designers themselves). An over-designed navigation bar displayed at miniature scale challenges your motor-coordination skills.

Ultima Online
http://www.uo.com

Like most PC-based online games, *Ultima* has failed to find a stylized visual grammar to complement its orthographic structure. The depressing results – tiresome medievalism in the service of a virtual world – are nevertheless unaccountably popular with legions of gamers who have famously turned the site into a sociopolitical test-tube. Plagued by incidents of rape and pillage by marauding players, the developers have continuously retooled the paid subscription game's parameters in much the same way as a real-world govern-ing body would adjust its laws and bylaws to maintain social order.

Vector Park
http://www.vectorpark.com

A small collection of interactive experiments created with the Flash plug-in by Patrick Smith includes a mysterious landscape to explore and an absorbing physics-based balancing game.

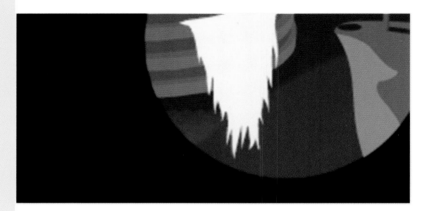

Vectorama.org
http://www.vectorama.org

Concocted by a trio of designers calling themselves Display Switzerland, this "multi-user playground" permits players to create a picture together by dragging vector-graphic elements from libraries and dropping them on a display. The items can be moved, scaled, rotated and colored, printed or sent as e-mail.

Volume One
http://www.volumeone.com

Matt Owen's much praised, obsessively detailed, quarterly showcase for the designer's graphic explorations is self-described as "a visual communications project dedicated to the exploration of new narrative possibilities."

The Web Standards Project
http://www.webstandards.org

A coalition of Web developers and users, the project's mission is to halt the fragmentation of the Web by persuading browser makers that a consistent set of standards is in both users' and developers' best interests. In the words of its creators, "Together we can make the Web accessible to all."

When I Am King
http://www.demian5.com

Swiss comic artist Damien Vogler's weekly installments of his epic, nonsensical graphic novella unspool in a series of horizontal scrolls – marked by a titillating story line rife with "naughty bits" – that play with ideas of time, motion and space.

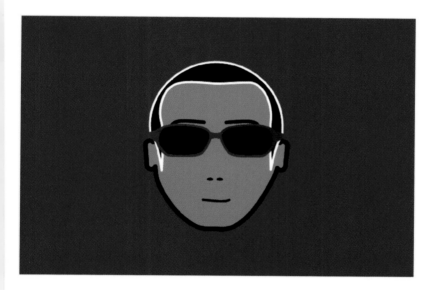

Jim Woodring
http://www.jimwoodring.com

A Seattle-based cartoonist, graphic-novelist and animator posts a gallery of his wonderfully deranged artwork, including a wildly surrealistic short movie.

GROUPS & EVENTS

Associations, conferences, competitions, festivals...

No respectable profession is complete without its clubs, which is why trade organizations that service a working membership have sprung up over the years to serve just about every niche of design practice. In the U.S. – a nation that is, historically, stingy when it comes to cultural matters – most professional groups are privately supported. In other countries the picture is strikingly different, with national governments stepping in to assume a leadership role. The Web has proved to be ideal for these largely non-profit entities, allowing low-cost avenues of fraternization with members and an unprecedented degree of cross-communication. Some groups have formalized the instantaneous feedback loop the Web permits with active bulletin boards that follow the threads of discourse reflecting their membership's concerns.

Meanwhile, aspiring and working designers are confronted with a bewildering array of organized events that only seem to multiply. Such gatherings offer an unrivalled opportunity for designers to escape the confines of their studios and see more of their colleagues, but while there's no substitute for meeting face-to-face, the Web has once again emerged to play a contributing role. The burgeoning presence of designers online has dispensed by and large with the necessity of travelling long distances – and paying stiff registration fees – to view what is now readily available in virtual form, and that also goes for hitherto well-nigh impossible-to-access work in motion graphics and multimedia.

GROUPS & EVENTS

After Effects Film Festival
http://www.aftereffectswest.com

Held in connection with After Effects West, a trade show for the software that is revolutionizing indie film production, the festival annually celebrates the best efforts of a host of student and professional contestants.

AIGA Conference on Design for Film and Television
http://www.aiga.org

The AIGA/DFTV, held annually in New York City, maps out the territory of this nascent profession, and introduces some of the key practitioners and commentators. The event "takes on the changing roles of the designer in the evolving field of time-related design, examines the current scene, and explores the relationship between those roles and that scene."

The American Center for Design
http://www.ac4d.org

Respected for the 100 Show, its critically acclaimed annual competition, Living Surfaces conferences and seminar series, the ACD has been reshuffled in recent years, in a quest to carry out its mission as "a primary source of information about design and its role in our culture and our economy." The group has historically played second fiddle to its larger cousin, the American Institute of Graphic Arts, but inherits a reputation for thoughtful and effective communication with its members.

American Film Institute
http://www.afionline.org

Unabashedly populist, the AFI is probably best known for its Life Achievement Awards and notorious 100-best lists. The Institute's annual Digital Arts Workshops, "created to address and stimulate artistic exploration in the emerging field of New Media" are more down-to-earth.

American Institute of Graphic Arts
http://www.aiga.org

Despite its 87-year history, 16,000 members and self-proclaimed mission of "stimulating thinking about design," the existence of the AIGA is pretty much a well-kept secret outside professional circles. Nevertheless, it's a my-way-or-the-highway proposition for most U.S. graphic designers. If you're not a member of the AIGA – with its pricey entry fees, its splashy headquarters and bewildering array of conferences, exhibitions, competitions and retreats – you're just not considered part of the club. The AIGA's biannual bash is the indisputable Big Kahuna of design conferences: the extravaganza attracts upward of 3,000 attendees. The Institute also holds smaller conferences that eschew the bread-and-circuses for more focused presentations on business and convergence. The site hosts *Loop*, a forum dealing with interactive design education.

American Society for Information Science and Technology
http://www.asis.org

Founded over 60 years ago, this U.S.-based professional organization declares it has, since then, been "*the* society for information professionals leading the search for new and better theories, techniques and technologies to improve access to information." An uninviting site doesn't provide much corroboration.

Art Directors Club
http://www.adcny.org

The prestigious New York City-based fraternal organization is well known for its monthly exhibitions and for raising awareness about magazine design. Members include creatives in advertising, graphic design, interactive media, broadcast design, typography, photography, illustration and related disciplines, but the old-boy network, through its Visual Fuel program, tries to reach out to students and professionals as well. The Club's phallocentric Hall of Fame numbers close to 100 but includes only half-a-dozen women.

Aspen International Design Conference
http://www.idca.org

The granddaddy of them all, the International Design Conference in Aspen (the "Spirit of Design") has suffered from an image problem in the last decade or so, amid the perception that it's run by an old-boy network and that later installments had lost their edge. That seems to have been turned around with recent gatherings, nods to digital design – and besides, the conference "where design matters" shows no sign of going away. Oh, and the setting helps.

Association of Independent Video and Filmmakers
http://www.aivf.org

AIVF was established by a group of independent filmmakers to offer support and resources to independent artists. Today, the Association is at the forefront of many media advocacy efforts, while serving individuals and the field at large through its commitment to supporting artists throughout their entire career.

Association of Professional Design Firms
http://www.apdf.org

The APDF is dedicated to elevating the standards of design and professional business practices for design consulting firms, giving them the ability to learn from each other by networking and openly sharing information.

British Academy of Film and Television Arts
http://www.bafta.org

BAFTA is Britain's leading organization promoting and rewarding the best in film, television and interactive media. Renowned for its high-profile award ceremonies covering film, TV, children's and interactive entertainment, the Academy sponsors a wide range of events which are not only open to Academy members, but to non-members as well.

British Design & Art Direction
http://www.dandad.org

A professional organization representing Britain's design and art direction community that is famous for its Yellow Pencil awards. The site posts a "blood bank" of links to young creative talent and hosts a Green Room for discussion.

British Film Institute
http://www.bfi.org.uk

The foremost repository for film lore in Britain posts schedules of film showings, information on its Museum of the Moving Image, access to collections and archives, with links to more film information, as well as news and features.

British Interactive Multimedia Association
http://www.bima.co.uk

BIMA, as the name implies, is the trade association representing the interactive media industries in Britain. The group sponsors multifarious activities and provides networking opportunities, offering information and support.

Broadcast Designers Association
http://www.bda.tv

A worldwide organization working on behalf of professionals involved in the promotion, marketing and design of all electronic media, from TV, radio and the Internet to video post-production, advertising and media consultancy, the BDA proposes "to raise the profile and quality of work produced by our industry, and to educate and inspire the next generation of creative talent." Members include senior executives, producers, editors, writers and the creators of advertising, graphics and publicity materials, representing more than 3,800 member companies and individuals throughout 70 countries. The Association's annual awards program in electronic media confers instant recognition on its winners.

The Center For Media Sciences

http://www.mediaguru.org

Founded to follow in the footsteps and further the exploration of the ideas of Marshall McLuhan, the father-figure of modern communications technology, the Center works to update and revitalize the great man's insights, seeking "to continue to scrutinize the interface between technology and culture; to 'project forward' using today's percepts; to analyze; to stimulate; to discuss; and to assist in the development of the science of media analysis."

Communications Research Institute

http://www.communication.org.au

A non-profit research group that helps organizations improve the user experience, CRI promises "a unique mix of practical services and research." The site posts a paper, "Experiences in Co-designing," that gives an insightful summary of the research process.

Creative Time

http://www.creativetime.org

The New York City-based non-profit arts advocacy program follows its dictum of "presenting art where you least expect it" by hosting multimedia installations and other art works in otherwise inhospitable locations.

Day Without Art

http://www.creativetime.org/dwa

The annual AIDS message project by Brooklyn-based Creative Time provides downloadable banners from an international roster of artists for you to post on your Web site, thus ensuring a spotlight on these spirited responses to the epidemic.

Design and Culture

http://www.designandculture.org

Aiming to portray "How Design Impacts The World As We Know It," this annual conference assembles an all-star line-up representing a spectrum of design disciplines. The event includes the usual "specialty" learning sessions, receptions and keynote speeches by design industry heavyweights.

Design Centre of the Czech Republic
http://www.designcentrum.cz

The sole online source for information about Czech domestic events and competitions suffers from marginal graphic content.

Design Council
http://www.designcouncil.org.uk

A British government-sponsored initiative to help produce and improve the aesthetics of the country's policies and services, the Council aims "to inspire the best use of design by the United Kingdom, in the world context, to improve prosperity and well-being."

Design Exchange
http://www.designexchange.org

The Toronto-based outfit bills itself as "the only design promotion centre of its kind in North America." A non-profit, educational organization sponsored by the Canadian government, the "DX," as it likes to be called, is committed to promoting an understanding of design by business and the general public. The site posts news of its ambitious exhibition, education and outreach programs.

DesignFilms
http://www.designfilms.org

Conceived as a vehicle for media culture studies, this educational resource is dedicated to promoting the digital design arts. The organization also sponsors a multimedia program devoted to the historical development of motion-picture title design that has toured to museum venues in major cities in the U.S. and Europe. The group hosts as well a series of annual showcases for contemporary title design. The site posts news of upcoming events and touring schedules.

The Design Management Institute
http://www.dmi.org

The DMI is a non-profit organization dedicated to demonstrating the strategic role of design in business, and to improving the management and utilization of design. The Institute's programs assist design managers in becoming leaders in their profession, and foster interaction among design managers, organizational managers, public policy-makers and academics. An extensive series of annual conferences aims to improve the general public's understanding of the nature, process and significance of design.

Doors of Perception
http://www.doorsofperception.nl

An international conference and disseminated knowledge network, the Amsterdam-based think-fest tables new agendas for design, with an eye to information and communication technologies. The site archives five years of past conferences, posting copious links as well as notices for the next installment.

Eyebeam Atelier

http://www.eyebeam.org

A relative newcomer, this New York City-based non-profit media-arts organization makes cutting-edge technology accessible to artists, students and children. Construction of a new museum and exhibition space is currently underway.

Eyes & Ears of Europe

http://www.eyesandears.net

A conference, awards and workshop program devoted to design, promotion, marketing, multimedia, TV and radio, the organization hosts activities held in Berlin and Cologne.

Filmmaker's Collaborative

http://www.filmmakers.org

The New York City-based facility provides an environment for independent producers and directors at an affordable price. The Collaborative is designed to create an open atmosphere where filmmakers have the opportunity to develop and realize projects through collective resources and open discussion.

5k

http://www.the5k.org

A competition held annually for excellence in Web design and production, the award comes with just one stipulation: the winning project must have a file size of 5K or less. According to the organizers, "the idea behind the contest is that the rigid constraints of designing for the Web are what force us to get [sic] truly creative."

Flashforward
http://www.flashforward2002.com

Geeks flock to this independently-produced, wildly popular educational and inspirational conference, dedicated to supporting the community of designers and developers who have gathered around Macromedia Flash and other products that "write" the SWF format. Presenters run the gamut from hardcore enthusiasts to artier types.

Fresh Conference
http://www.freshconference.com

With an emphasis on encouraging the sharing of ideas among an achingly hip roster of top Web design professionals from around the world, this lively Pacific Rim-oriented conference aims to "inspire, educate and empower participants with new ideas and directions, as well as provide a deeper insight into fast-developing Web technology."

Graphic Artists Guild
http://www.gag.org

The national union of U.S. illustrators, designers, Web creators, production artists, surface designers and other creatives encourages its members "to pursue common goals, share their experience, raise industry standards, and improve the ability of visual creators to achieve satisfying and rewarding careers." Esteemed for its *Handbook of Pricing & Ethical Guidelines,* the Guild has worked to improve the profession's standing through democratic and egalitarian means, within a structure open to all working artists.

Houyhnhnms
http://www.houyhnhnms.org

In what is billed as a "Flash Global Inspirational Experiment," programmers and designers from around the world are invited to submit works executed in the wildly popular animation format as part the OFFF Flash Film Festival based in Barcelona.

HOW Design Conference
http://www.howconference.com

Sagely recognizing that "graphic design is a business as well as an art," this annual four-day event sponsored by the print magazine provides a hands-on, educational program to enable designers to balance better the three key components of graphic design: creativity, business and technology. Conference sessions cover a mix of these critical design issues, with particular emphasis on creative and business topics. HOW's conferences have won respect for their hands-on, nuts-and-bolts approach and student-friendly prices and structure. Just don't expect a lot of fireworks.

The Illustration Conference
http://www.illustconf.org

Committed to "providing a stage for an ongoing dialogue that serves the whole industry," this annual get-together attracts the cream of the illustration crop, providing a platform for illustrators to address the most pervasive, timely ideas and to tackle issues – like copyright theft – of vital interest to the profession.

Image and Meaning
http://web.mit.edu/i-m/conference.htm

Envisioning and communicating science and technology, the Massachusetts Institute of Technology sponsors this annual event, "launched to help scientists and science communicators develop and share improved methods of communicating technical information through images linked to appropriate text." The conference's goal is to enhance the level of discourse within the scientific community, and among teachers and those who communicate with the public through the mass media.

International Animated Film Society Festlist
http://www.asifa.org/animate/festlist.htm

The society's site includes listings and links to animation festivals worldwide.

International Association of Web Masters and Designers
http://www.iawmd.com

Founded by and for Web professionals, the IT-oriented Association is dedicated to "creating a clear, collected voice of the membership, regarding ethics, principles and standards of business on the Internet." A grimly utilitarian presentation on the site underscores its seriousness.

International Browser Day

http://www.internationalbrowserday.com

This annual slugfest invites designers, programmers and others to adapt the browser model to "redraw the face of the future from a design and user-centric perspective." Still going strong – despite waning prospects for a paradigm shift – the competition looks for "breakthrough concepts, new ways of seeing, and using the Internet in an undefined context of 21st-century design and communications."

International Festival New Cinema New Media

http://www.fcmm.com

This three-day event, held in Montreal, includes a juried competition and awards to a roster of largely obscure new-media artists. An online festival makes the case for relevance.

International Professional Publishers Association

http://www.ippa.org

Self-described as "the Web's leading design association," the IPPA was founded as an association of design and technology professionals working in new media and the Web, with the role to "foster quality solutions for commercial applications of the Internet." The association also provides a forum for communication and discussions about the future of the Internet, e-commerce, e-business and the digital revolution.

Living Surfaces

http://www.ac4d.org

Organized by the American Center for Design and originated to provide a forum on interactive media for leading design practitioners and educators, this annual gathering is recognized as the first conference to focus on the Internet as a rapidly growing design venue. Presenters each year explore a specific topic or theme relating to the changing landscape of interactive media and its relation to design.

133

Macworld Conference & Expo
http://www.macworldexpo.com

The bicoastal (New York City and San Francisco) showcase for products and services geared to professionals and consumers involved in traditional and new media, creative content development and home applications. The conference leverages the loyal base of Mac OS audiences in creative services, education, consumer applications, entertainment, small office/home and Internet-based environments.

National Film Board of Canada
http://www.nfb.ca

A jewel in the Canadian cultural crown for the past 60 years, the NFB is a government agency that produces and distributes films and other audiovisual works, and serves as the storehouse for a large part of the country's cinematic heritage. Throughout its lifetime, the NFB has been associated with some of the most remarkable technical and artistic breakthroughs in film production, especially animation. A proficient site posts news of recent documentaries and shorts in release with a catalog of videos you can order. A few clips would have been nice.

New Media Centre
http://www.newmediacentre.com

A project of London's Institute of Contemporary Art, the center is dedicated to digital art. The site posts screensavers, online digital art projects and links to kindred spirits.

New York New Media Association
http://www.nynma.org

Founded "to serve the entrepreneur, creative and business professional, and promote the industry as it grows in New York," the NYNMA works to promote the city's Silicon Alley district as a leading center of an emerging industry.

No Todo Film Fest
http://www.plus.es/codigo/notodo/index.asp

Boasting the not-so-surprising distinction of being "the first Spanish festival made exclusively for the Internet," this annual event caters to the new generation of Web-savvy filmmakers. The movies must be submitted in either AVI, MPEG, Flash, QuickTime or RealVideo formats, no more than 3.5 MB per file. The site humorously presents the concept of compression behind the restrictions on entries.

OneDotZero

http://www.onedotzero.com

O

This London-based festival is a real-world annual event intended to showcase the creative possibilities of desktop digital filmmaking. The site charts the festival's role in the commissioning, programming and producing of work that involves the digital moving image, as well as in developing cross-media and interactive projects including CD-ROMs, print, the Internet, TV and installations.

100 Show

http://www.ac4d.org/events/ev_100show.asp

The American Center for Design's prestigious annual competition has a reputation for awarding edgy, handsome work in graphic design. The show's unusual format – rather than labor toward a consensus, jurors present their individual choices – guarantees an idiosyncratic mix of winners.

Presenting Data and Information

http://www.edwardtufte.com

P

The near-legendary one-day course taught by information design guru Edward Tufte regularly tours major U.S. cities. Even if you've already been awed and inspired by the great man's books, you shouldn't miss this presentation. The site doesn't add anything to the discussion, but helpfully posts current tour dates.

PROMAX

http://www.bda.tv

Advertised as "the world's largest gathering of promotion, marketing and design professionals in TV, digital media and radio," this annual event brings together thousands of producers, designers and senior executives for what's claimed to be the world's largest "educative" forum for the exchange of information, experience and ideas in the promotion, marketing and design industry.

RESFEST

http://www.resfest.com

R

Organized by the RES Media Group, RESFEST is an annual touring celebration of digital film that features screenings, panels and technology demonstrations. The program's curators have an unerring eye for imaginative, groundbreaking work and the show is a chance to see seldom-screened masterworks from an international pool of talent.

Shonan World Design Awards
http://www.design-award.com

An Internet design competition, the Awards are held annually to support the development of digital arts, and to contribute to an international exchange of artists.

Siggraph
http://www.siggraph.org

Now approaching its 30th year, this international conference on computer graphics and interaction – held annually in Los Angeles – is really just a big old ugly trade show, but it's such an industry heavyweight that it's impossible to ignore. N-Space, a gallery devoted to "digitally based and inspired artwork," is consistently disappointing.

Slamdance
http://www.slamdance.com/2002

The pierced-and-tattooed, rebellious younger sibling of the Park City, Utah-based Sundance Festival – independent moviedom's Holy Grail – fosters work by first-time filmmakers. The feature competition is devoted to films by first-time directors who have made films that do not have domestic distribution or hefty budgets. Slamdance "welcomes films in any subject matter, length, format (including digital and video), finished or not."

The Society for Information Display
http://www.sid.org

Members of the SID are professionals in all of the technical and business disciplines that relate to display research, design, manufacturing, applications, marketing and sales, "developing and manufacturing the displays for the 21st century, and applying them to exciting information, telecommunications, medical, commercial, government, entertainment, and consumer products."

The Society for News Design
http://www.snd.org

Well-known for its annual Best of Newspaper Design competition, the SND is an international professional organization with more than 2,500 members, comprised of editors, designers, graphic artists, publishers, illustrators, art directors, photographers, advertising artists, Web site designers, students and faculty.

The Society of Publication Designers
http://www.spd.org

Billed as "the only organization specifically addressing the concerns of trade, institutional, newspaper and consumer editorial art directors," the SPD annually judges the work of thousands of design professionals in the U.S. and around the world to come up with its well-publicized awards.

Streaming Cinema
http://www.streamingcine.com

A festival of Web-centric films (with the caveat that "it isn't film anymore") produced by The Bit Screen, a New York City-based promoter, this digital showcase tours annually, in late summer and early fall, to major cities around the world. "Cinema is an art form rooted in technology – the result of the interplay between technology and art," the organizers say. "So films created for the Web are fundamentally different [from] theatrical cinema. These Web films are really laying the groundwork for the future of film."

Sushi
http://www.adc-sushi.de

The Frankfurt-based German Art Directors Club hosts this handsome showcase (no English text) for individual artists, illustrators and assorted other creatives honored in its annual competition.

TED
http://www.ted.com

Founded with the observation that the "three primary communications-driven business and professional areas in our society were emerging, merging and evolving together in ways undreamed of just a few short years before," the annual TED Conferences attract major movers-and-shakers from the fields of technology, entertainment and design (thus the acronym). Famously expensive and hard to get into, TED has waned in influence in recent years, but the event still represents a touchstone "for understanding the nature of late 20th-century communications."

Typecon
http://www.typecon.com

The annual typography conference organized by a group whimsically known as the Society of Typographic Aficionados holds its proceedings in un-trendy Rochester, New York, but attracts an international roster of type celebrities.

TypeRight
http://www.typeright.org

An ad-hoc group composed of a diverse crew of type designers, developers, type foundries and aficionados, "working together to promote typefaces as creative works and to advocate their legal protection as intellectual property."

Typomedia
http://www.typomedia.com

Held every summer in Mainz, Germany, this typography conference attracts internationally renowned speakers on the topics of design, typography, calligraphy, advertising, art, photography, TV, printing, the Internet, science and media technology. The gathering strives to address the latest developments in media, design and communication, with the idea that "static and dynamic media are seeking new forms of expression and everything is in a state of flux."

Uppsala International Short Film Festival
http://shortfilmfestival.com

Now into its 20th year, the esteemed Finnish showcase for cinematic exploration is held in the fall.

V-2 Organization
http://www.v-2.org

Self-described as the "third millennium design lab," this British think-tank for issues related to information design and usability, media and culture posts brainy articles, and lots of up-to-date listings and gossip.

Web Sites that Work
http://world.std.com/~uieweb/courses.htm

An outfit known as User Interface Engineering offers a number of pricey one- and two-day courses, based on usability studies of real sites, at locations near Boston, Seattle, Austin and San Francisco.

Webby Awards
http://www.webbyawards.com

Presented by the International Academy of Digital Arts and Sciences, and held each summer in San Francisco, "the Oscars of the Internet" honors Web sites in a plethora of categories, with a nod to projects devoted to art and film. The ceremony's People's Voice Awards lends an egalitarian note.

Web2002
http://www.web2002show.com

The official conference of *Web Techniques* magazine and WebReview.com, WEB2002 is billed as "the premier conference for Web professionals."

SERVICES

Suppliers, vendors, communities...

While it's true that companies trying to make money exclusively on the Web have frequently crashed and burned, quite a few paid online resources for designers are hanging in there. Offering their services for hire, most vendors and suppliers are savvy enough to be look-up-able by a dedicated search, so we've confined our selection to the noteworthy and exceptional.

If the Internet hadn't come along, stock photo agencies would have to have invented it. Selecting a photograph and getting it delivered, traditionally a huge headache for creators and providers, used to take weeks; now the process can be completed in mere minutes. Users can search, purchase and download an image in real time instead of sorting through bound catalogs and waiting for couriers to arrive.

Type foundries have successfully seized the opportunities the Web provides for ease of access and streamlined ordering. While some foundries that post significant editorial content are included in "Media" and "Practice" sections, those listed here focus almost exclusively on handling your order, in some cases developing highly customized responses to customers' tastes and preferences.

Adobe Systems
http://www.adobe.com

The software monster's corporate presence online is leavened with in-depth tutorials and quick tips for Web, print and digital video professionals; galleries and interviews with world-class designers and filmmakers; technical information; community forums, and more. The site makes it inordinately difficult to find them, forcing you to slog through a lot of product literature to get there.

Alphabets, Inc.
http://www.alphabets.com

Online showings of a superior range of typefaces are tastefully and imaginatively displayed. "Fonts for the information age" can be viewed as animated GIFs, in Flash animations or as PDF downloads. The company also distributes the International Typefounders CD-ROM, with more than 3,000 fonts from 30-plus leading independent foundries.

Argus Center for Information Architecture
http://argus-acia.com

According to its presentable but no-nonsense site, this U.S. consultancy "provides leadership in defining and advancing the evolving discipline of information architecture." Besides offering its services online, ACIA posts a selective collection of links to notable content, events and people in the field; original articles, white papers, conferences and seminars that draw from the experience and expertise of the Argus team; and research, independently and through partnerships, focused on improving collective understanding of information architecture.

Corbis
http://www.corbis.com

Billed as "the definitive destination for photography and fine art in the digital age," the Corbis Collection – enviably bankrolled by none other than Microsoft – contains some of the world's most significant photography and fine art. With more than 65 million images, more than two million of them online, Corbis offers a wide range of choice and is the leading provider of digital images to both the consumer and creative professional markets. The company uses its extensive Internet technology to allow customers to quickly and conveniently access and purchase images and related products.

Creative HotList
http://www.creativehotlist.com

A workaday feature of *Communication Arts* magazine's family of Web sites focused on job listings for graphic design professionals, this "customizable online application" for connecting talent, companies and services is difficult to assess. Whether it's a usable service or mere promotional tool depends on your viewpoint.

CyberWorld
http://www.cyberworldcorp.com

A commercial venture with some intriguing possibilities, this "rich media" developmental tool allows designers to seamlessly integrate multimedia products into a 3D environment without modeling or tedious programming. Designers can build virtual environments from a kit of parts that allows customers to "walk the Web in 3D," in what is, hopefully, a lifelike and interactive online experience.

D

DV Creators
http://www.dvcreators.net

Billed as "the market leader in digital media training," the service offers instruction and resources for digital video production. "Our workshops and products put you on the fast track to achieving your dreams with Desktop Movies, whether you're a marketing executive, teacher, DV filmmaker, trainer, Web designer, graphics artist or simply someone with a story to tell."

Dynamic Graphics
http://www.dgusa.com

An unassuming site offers stock photos and footage, practical advice, easy-to-follow instructions and creative techniques for corporate and graphic communications teams.

E

Eyestorm
http://www.eyestorm.com

In the already crowded field of online retail arts sales, where schlock of every description abounds, Eyestorm offers real value to the serious and well-informed contemporary art and photography collector. Niche marketing at its best, it's billed as a "place to discover, explore and acquire contemporary art and photography." The site hawks limited editions by a roster of blue-chip artists and photographers. The substantial editorial content provided by a small stable of talented scribes is articulate, even erudite, and refreshingly tough-minded. It's fleshed out with announcements of exhibitions worldwide featuring member artists. If you're looking for a convenient handle on what's happening in the art world or just shopping for the trendiest art objects on the Web, you could do much, much worse.

Faces

http://www.iqbiometrix.com

Its developers encourage you to "think of Faces as police sketch artist software for the new millennium." Scary enough? By simply clicking on easy-to-read icons, users of all ages can create billions of faces of all ages, either sex or any race from a bank of about 4,000 facial features. You can send composites you create to your friends (and of your friends, if you so desire) by e-mail or fax. Reportedly, the software is being used to train kids to recognize assailants – social engineering at its finest.

Fine Art in Print

http://www.fineartinprint.com

This New York City-based purveyor of books on graphic design and typography, architecture and criticism posts an eclectic selection of featured titles from the foreign to the obscure.

FontShop

http://www.fontshop.com

Founded by type aficionados Erik Spiekermann and Neville Brody, Berlin-based FontShop International posts an electronic edition of its celebrated FontFont typeface specimen at this crisply detailed site. There are currently 1,700 FontFonts which cover a wide range of styles and functions, including some wildly uninhibited display fonts, a tasteful selection of high-quality text faces, symbol sets, Cyrillic typefaces and "intelligent" fonts such as the notorious RandomFonts that morph on command.

For Designers

http://www.fordesigners.com

While primarily a showcase for the sale of fonts, photography, clip art and illustration by Connecticut-based DsgnHaus, this site also posts articles from the defunct *X-Height* print magazine.

The Foundry

http://www.thefoundrystudio.co.uk

A low-key presentation for British designers David Quay and Freda Sack, producers and distributors of the "internationally renowned" eight-font-strong Foundry typeface range.

French Paper Company
http://www.frenchpaper.com

A "design resource" that unapologetically hawks the company's products online offers swatches and promotions, ordering, clip art and a collection of retro fonts.

 ## Getty Images
http://www.gettyimages.com

With an archive of more than 70 million still images and – a new feature – approximately 30,000 hours of stock film, Getty Images has recast itself as an "e-commerce provider of imagery," making it perhaps the largest corporation mining the vast landscape of visual content. The world's leading "footage brands" are only a click away in the motion section at this inviting site. Use fast keyword searches to preview motion clips, download easy-to-edit scenes and screen the freshest footage.

 ## Habbo Hotel
http://www.habbohotel.com

Sporting a distinctive and surprisingly ingratiating graphic identity, this London-based venture appears to be a stylistic twin of the charming Mobiles Disco (see "Projects"). Following the model of virtual "chat worlds" elsewhere, you create your own custom personality, then you venture forth into the hotel's various public and private rooms, communicating with the other denizens by e-mail messaging. In this dauntingly complex parallel universe, you're encouraged to purchase your own inner sanctum, furnishing it from a shopping list of amusing bric-a-brac.

Human Factors International
http://www.humanfactors.com

Promising "we make software usable" from a grimly efficient site, this user-centered systems integration company aims to improve the interactions that people have with computers by offering end-to-end software solutions for Web intranet and Internet-based applications. The company also works to help make clients' existing software more friendly and efficient for customers, other clients and employees.

Indie 7
http://www.indie7.com

This online resource for independent filmmakers looks slightly underdeveloped. There's an industry directory, "cool resources" and show business news.

Information Architects
http://www.iarchitect.com

The public face of Isys Information Architects, a full-service provider of user interface design and usability engineering services, isn't much to look at but it is chock-full of helpful pointers and sobering instruction. Reminding us that "careful attention to the user interface can reduce system development time, increase user satisfaction and reduce training costs," the company posts an Interface Hall of Fame – and a Hall of Shame that's fascinating for its tips on what not to do when battling for viewers' eyeballs.

International Typeface Corporation
http://www.itcfonts.com

An international leader in typeface design and marketing for more than 25 years, ITC collaborates with world-class designers to provide a library of more than 1,000 classic typefaces and innovative new designs. Firmly in the mainstream of type marketing, the company claims to have helped raise the standards of design quality, and focused attention on the ethical issues related to design protection and licensing for typography. The site maintains an online version of the company's late, much-lamented print version of *U&lc* magazine.

The I-spot Showcase
http://www.theispot.com

Billed as "illustration Internet site" I-spot boasts an online directory that integrates a wide variety of sophisticated search features. You can search by category, artist or keyword (subject, style, medium) to discover a very mixed bag of highly commercial illustration.

L

LifeF/X software
http://www.lifefx.com

Touted as next-generation Ana Nova-type technology, LifeF/X develops software products and services that enable users to communicate through photo-realistic, digital images of human faces that can speak, move and show emotion. Its proprietary software platform consists of a player with an embedded text-to-speech engine and a facial animation system. By typing text onto a computer screen and selecting from a range of emotions, customers can use its software to transmit a spoken, animated message across the Internet. It's a risky business model, but LifeF/X hopes to put a personalized face on online communications such as Web sites and e-mail.

The List
http://webdesign.thelist.com

"The definitive buyer's guide to Web design" lists thousands of designers offering Web services worldwide and several hundred studios in California alone, none of which – on a random pass – we'd ever heard of.

M

Magma Books
http://www.magmabooks.com or http://www.rarefuel.com

A relative newcomer, this London retail and exhibition space hosts a hip site that doesn't shrink from merchandising many of the more outré contributions to publishing in the fields of graphic design, architecture, photography and fashion. It also sells its own specially commissioned limited-edition posters and prints, CD-ROMs, DVDs and other design-related products through the site.

MyFonts
http://myfonts.com

With more than 14,000 fonts grouped into 4,000-plus families, MyFonts makes it easy to browse and purchase the latest type fashions. Want a "casual friendly" look? Type that in and up comes a serving of fonts fitting the description. Ever wanted to have a font just like the one used by certain publications, corporations or ad campaigns? Using the WhatTheFont font recognition system, you can upload a scanned image of the font and MyFonts will show you the closest matches in its database. Yet another trippy feature, Type Xplorer lets you compare fonts by bold, width, contrast and x-height settings.

Nielsen Norman Group
http://www.nngroup.com

Founded by the two grand curmudgeons of interface design, Jakob Nielsen and Donald A. Norman, and recently joined by Apple interface veteran Bruce "Tog" Tognazzini, the consulting group offers "strategies to enhance the user experience." The members of Nielsen Norman Group are user experience pioneers who, they are at pains to remind us, advocated user-centered design and usability well before it became popular to do so. Besides catering to industry clients, the trio tour extensively with a program designed to debunk the sacred shibboleths of overly arty design direction.

Nijhof & Lee
http://www.nijhoflee.nl

Dealers in new and out-of-print books in the fields of art, architecture, design and photography, this Amsterdam-based bookseller focuses in particular on graphic design, exhibition catalogues and reference works. The site includes a sales gallery of unusual and provocative posters by Dutch designers.

Pictoplasma
http://www.pictoplasma.com

Advertising itself as a source for contemporary human and animal character designs, Pictoplasma celebrates the richly-endowed art of creature imagery with links to roughly 200 largely foreign, established and up-and-coming artists worldwide. The service – with a dialed-down palette that provides a discreet backdrop for its wares – links to a roster of astonishingly high quality 2D and 3D, vector- and pixel-based digital illustration. For the impatient, an exhibitions section quickly serves up clues to the contents, and the archives helpfully categorize by artist name, country of origin, style, and – yes – types of characters.

Scopeware
http://www.scopeware.com

Programming guru David Gelernter developed this intriguing but somewhat mysterious software as an elegant alternative to the current desktop – an interface that, in his view, is still mired in a bygone era when megabytes were scarce and CPUs lethargic. Scopeware provides a paradigm-shifting patented information management infrastructure that manages, customizes and delivers your personal information irrespective of its source, automatically and in real time. A design-challenged presentation on the site doesn't help matters however, and the actual look and feel of the stuff remains maddeningly elusive.

The Sims
http://thesims.ea.com/us

The developers of *Sim City* had a huge hit on their hands almost overnight, creating online environments for a community of users who grew addicted to manipulating the economies of their respective realms. Spurred on by *Sim City*'s phenomenal success, its creators launched this virtual soap opera in the form of a version of the old game that is populated by actual characters.

Tony Stone
http://www.tonystone.com

Promising somewhat illogically "to create exceptional, contemporary photography for the advertising and design industry" (isn't that what photographers do?), this well-respected and long-established stock service claims to generate some 60 innovative new images every day, delivered from lens to desktop in up-to-the-minute fashion via high-quality RGB scans. A good place to find some of the edgier and more memorable stock images out there.

William Stout Architectural Books
http://www.stoutbooks.com

This San Francisco-based bookseller specializes in the building arts, but its inventory of graphic design publishing is unrivalled. The site advertises a retail database that records not just stock, but every title that has passed through the store in the last few years.

T Thinkmap
http://www.thinkmap.com

Developed by New York City-based Plumb Design, ThinkMap provides a remarkably original "authoring platform" that organizes information online in real time, according to a relational database. Unlike conventional database front-ends that are grounded in displaying lists of information, a range of proprietary applications encourages dynamic exploration of data sources. In action, the program allows you to push and pull at a site map of information sources that constantly shifts to accommodate new relationships according to your preferences. By engaging data in this way, users hopefully discover unexpected connections and interrelationships that aren't immediately apparent with conventional browsing.

Turbo Squid
http://www.turbosquid.com

This worldwide 3D rendering database establishes a direct link between digital artists and those in search of digital content, from 3D models and textures to sound effects. By allowing artists to publish and promote their own assets quickly and easily, TurboSquid enables a rapid accumulation of digital media. The ability to dynamically search the entire database allows the user to easily compare different items using previews, written descriptions and even specific technical information.

Image © Turbo Squid, Inc Reprinted with Permission

Urbanpixel
http://www.urbanpixel.com

U

Advertising "breakthrough technology for visualizing, navigating and organizing complex information," Urbanpixel is a technology innovator and services company that aims to lead the way in providing the next generation (that phrase again) Web experience. To that end, the firm has assembled a team of industry experts in strategy, user experience design, software development and management from leading technology companies.

WebMap
http://www.webmap.com

W

The service was founded in response to "mounting frustration among businesses and individual users regarding the inefficiency of finding and accessing information," a felt need to be sure. The solution: provide software based upon a breakthrough in information mapping technology that makes interaction with the Internet, intranets, extranets and wireless technology through a visual rather than textual format. Unfortunately, less than compelling iterations have the effect of making the prospects of such an interface paradigm somewhat less than appealing.

APPENDIX

APPENDIX

Notes on Search

This book marks an attempt to catalog and assess as many Web sites as possible that might prove valuable to designers and those interested in design. Which is not to say there aren't some that we missed or that might be of interest to individual readers. Also beyond the scope of this book is the vast network of commerce that has proliferated online. To access these and other useful destinations you will need to search for them.

Unfortunately, the majority of designers – like most people – know very little about conducting a proper search. But while there are several schools of thought on search techniques, the ground rules are pretty basic. Unless you're making a scientific inquiry, you only need to know a few tips that consistently yield usable results. In their short lifetime, search engines have markedly improved in their ability to help sharpen the focus of your query and many now provide an "Are you looking for . . ." category that groups rough guesses about what you're after. Still, a few basics are in order.

Much depends, first and foremost, on the quality of your search engine, and here you need to be aware of a few basic truths. First of all, not all search engines are created equal. Not only that, the search engines you've probably heard the most about – at so called "portals" like Yahoo, Excite and Lycos – are, frankly, the least likely to be helpful. Search engines at the most popular sites are constructed like directories, their information filtered to provide what someone else thinks you may want to know. Which means that, if you're looking for material on the relatively arcane topic of design, the most popular search engines won't have much to offer. At the same time, you don't want to miss any potential information sources. That's why your search engine of choice should be a metasearcher – one that searches other search engines.

My favorite workaday search engine is the metasearcher GoTo (http://www.go2net.com), which is fine for a particular kind of search. I say "particular" because it's a second basic truth that search engines come in different flavors. Thus, GoTo easily finds home sites for groups, institutions and organizations that want you to find them. It has been built to cater to popular demand. Elsewhere, customized search engines are especially useful. If you're looking for a certain book, Amazon (http://www.amazon.com) provides an excellent resource (and that now goes for other formats besides books as well). If you're looking up something about movies, the Internet Movie Database (http://www.imdb.com), with its invaluable cross-references, offers a unique service.

If your needs are more academic, and you'd like an exhaustive listing of all the references to a certain topic, or even a specific name or phrase, then you will want to opt for Google (http://www.google.com). This modern wonder, in case you haven't heard, is affectionately viewed as the "mother" of all search engines by its millions of devoted users. With its famously minimal interface, Google cuts to the chase, coughing up so much stuff – a typical search yields 20 pages or so of listings – you're almost certain to find more on a given topic than you ever wanted to know. What makes Google so valuable is its ability – thanks to unique intelligence technology that ranks pages by how many other pages link to them – to organize information according to its overall relevance to the topic. This invaluable tool was recently made even more useful with the introduction of a date range searching function.

But wait, there's more. In the last year, Google has added a feature that promises to greatly enhance the way we view the Web. Not content to be the search engine of choice, the service recently juiced its offering with an image search function (http://images.google.com) that scrutinizes some quarter-billion potential matches and has quickly become a favorite tool among the design digerati. To capture them, Google analyzes the text on the page adjacent to the image, its caption, and dozens of other factors to determine the picture's content, using sophisticated algorithms to remove duplicates and ensure that the highest-quality images are presented first in your results. A search on isamu noguchi, for example, turned up hundreds of photos of the protean sculptor/designer and his works, shown as thumbnails that jump to a page where the image is captured – in a split screen – on its source page, as well as at its original displayed size.

As you refine your search skills, you'll learn that nuances in the way you phrase your query can have a major impact on the quality of your results. This learning process requires a certain amount of trial-and-error, especially since some strategies would appear to be counter-intuitive. For instance, if you're looking for stories about the great film title designer Saul Bass's career in Hollywood, you're better off with a search on saul bass than saul bass+hollywood. The latter query will generally yield a lot of irrelevant information on the world's movie capital.

A final word of warning. If you misspell or mislabel your query, what you've learned here will be wasted.

Happy hunting. – K.C.

GLOSSARY

Acronyms, jargon, slang

This guide provides definitions of generic terms which are frequently used in the text that are either specific to the Web or whose traditional meaning has been changed or modulated to some degree in the context of Web usage. It also includes explanations of widely used short forms of longer phrases that often confuse users.

A

ASCII *(American Standard Code for Information Interchange)* – The universally accepted standard for code numbers used by computers to represent upper- and lower-case letters, numbers, punctuation, etc.

audio loop – Brief sound recordings that repeat continuously.

B

blog *(bulletin log)* – An archive of written responses to a Web site.

C

cam – Live online feed from a video camera.

D

database – A collection of information organized so that its contents can be easily accessed, managed and updated. On a Web site, information from a database can be retrieved and presented in a browser by means of templates.

F

FTP *(file transfer protocol)* – The high-level Internet standard protocol for transferring files from one computer to another.

G

gateway – An interface that connects two different networks.

GIF *(graphics interchange format)* – A universal format with an economical file size developed for reading images on the Web.

GUI *(graphic user interface)* – All the visual elements of an interactive Web display.

H

home page Originally meant the Web page that your browser is set to use when it starts up. Now also refers to the main Web page for a business, organization or person, or simply the main page out of a collection of Web pages.

HTML *(hypertext markup language)* – The coding vocabulary used to make linking documents on the Web.

HTTP *(hypertext transfer protocol)* – The protocol for moving hypertext files across the Internet. Requires a HTTP client program on one end, and an HTTP server program on the other end. HTTP is the most important protocol used in the Web.

hub – A Web site consisting mainly of links to other sites.

hypertext – Text on the Web in which links to other sources are imbedded.

I

interface – A graphical surface that forms a common boundary between Web providers and users.

Internet – The vast collection of inter-connected networks that all use the TCP/IP protocols.

intranet – A private network inside a company or organization that uses the same software as the public Internet, but is exclusively for internal use.

ISDN *(Integrated Services Digital Network)* – A system that moves data more rapidly than modems over existing regular phone lines.

ISP *(Internet service provider)* – A paid service that provides access to the Internet.

J

JPEG *(Joint Photographic Experts Group)* – Named for the consortium that developed it. An image compression format that substantially reduces the size of image files with slightly reduced image quality and is superior to GIFs.

L

link – An element in the chain of Web connections, usually written in HTML.

M

message board – An online bulletin board where users can post their written communication.

morph – Change shape, color or size. Often, on the Web, by implementing animation software.

mouse-over – Action of using the hand-held remote control to activate interactive elements on the computer screen.

P

PDF *(portable document format)* – Enables documents with complex text and graphics to be viewed and printed on various computer platforms and systems with all information imbedded in the file.

plug-in – A program that can be quickly and easily installed, then used as part of a Web browser to enable additional or enhanced functions.

pop-up – A graphical user interface element, usually a small window, that appears in response to a mouse or cursor click or rollover.

portal – Any stopping-off point on the Internet that helps users navigate the online world. Many mainstream Web sites have been transformed into portals, offering stocks, sports and the like in predigested formats in hopes of becoming the main point of entry to a large audience.

Q

Quicktime Multimedia – format for displaying sound, text, animation and video in a single file.

R

rich media – Multimedia solutions that allow advertisers to implement e-commerce, lead generation and branding campaigns directly within their online banner ads.

rollover – Operation that involves moving a mouse or cursor over a given page element, resulting in a new display or action.

S

Shockwave – Add-on or plug-in that allows users to access compressed animations on the Web.

shovelware – Content with little or no real purpose or value posted online to give the appearance of editorial substance.

splash page – Opening screen used to present general information such as browser or plug-in requirements that often serves to distract the user while the required files are being downloaded.

streaming media – Technology accessed by downloadable plug-ins that allows you to view animations and listen to sound online for short periods of time.

Style sheets – Allow documents in an XML format to be easily converted into HTML.

T

TCP *(transmission control protocol)* – The Internet transport level protocol that provides reliable, full-duplex stream service upon which many application protocols rely.

TCP/IP *(transmission control protocol/Internet protocol)* – The suite of protocols that defines the Internet.

thread – A series of written messages and responses on an online bulletin board.

thumbnail – A reproduction at reduced size of an image displayed elsewhere on a linked Web page.

U

UI *(user interface)* – A common boundary between provider and user that conceivably has no graphical element. See also GUI.

URL or url *(uniform resource locator)* – The standard way to give the address of any resource on the Internet that is part of the World Wide Web.

usability – The aspect of interactive design that deals with user-oriented experience versus a top-down approach from provider to user.

V

vector graphics – Advanced programming that allows Web pages to be custom-enlarged to appear sharp at any magnification.

viral – Used to describe a marketing campaign or similar strategy that is disseminated by users themselves.

VRML *(virtual reality markup language)* – Programming designed to enable online 3D graphics and rendering.

W

Web or WWW *(World Wide Web)* – Loosely, the entire constellation of resources that can be accessed using various formats and other tools. Also refers to the universe of hypertext servers that allow text, graphics, sound files, etc. to be mixed together. Frequently used incorrectly when referring to "the Internet."

X

XML *(extensible markup language)* – Programming that allows documents to be coded to identify any desired portion of a document.

Legend

Most Web destinations contain some links to other sites, while others consist primarily or even exclusively of links to relevant material. These latter sites, here referred to as "hubs," are indicated throughout the text with an oversized colored asterisk.

INDEX

INDEX

167